مَدْخَلُ أَهْلِ الفِقْهِ وَاللِّسَانِ
إِلَى مَيْدَانِ المَحَبَّةِ وَالعِرْفَانِ

Madkhal Ahl al-Fiqh wal-Lisān
Ilā Maydān al-Maḥabbat wal-ʿIrfān

Inauguration of the Jurist and Linguist
into the Gardens of Love and Gnosis

Aḥmad b. Ibrāhīm al-Wāsiṭī
Ibn Shaykh al-Ḥazzāmiyyīn
(657-711H)

Translation
Abū Ibrāhīm John Starling

1st Edition, Ramaḍān 1441 | May 2020

ISBN: 9798666544730

Table of Contents

بسم الله الرحمن الرحيم

In the name of Allāh, Most Beneficent, Most Merciful.

Preface & Acknowledgements

All praise belongs to Allāh and may peace and prayers by upon our beloved Prophet, his family, companions, and all that follow his way until the Last Day.

As a holistic faith, the teachings of Islām are concerned with purifying both man's inner-self and outward actions. The Prophet ﷺ, in his comprehensive and inspired words, captured this notion in a narration collected by Imām Aḥmad which states, "Indeed Allāh The Mighty and Majestic does not look at your shapes and wealth, but looks at your hearts and deeds".

Paraphrasing from Ibn Rajab al-Ḥanbali, the heart acts as the king commanding his army, the limbs. If the king is upright, the army will be righteous. If the king is corrupt, the army will be evil. The same goes for the heart. If it is corrupt, the actions will be evil.

The Prophet ﷺ indicated this very sentiment in a narration collected by Imāms al-Bukhāri and Muslim which states, "Beware! There is a piece of flesh in the body that if reformed the whole body becomes reformed and if it gets spoilt the whole body gets spoilt and that is the heart".

Thus, focusing on the heart is of paramount importance for the faithful. Ridding the heart of evil and temptation will lead to sincere faith, dedicated devotion to the Divine, and impeccable manners with one's surroundings. Ridding the heart of disease is what will ultimately lead to salvation.

Allāh says what means, "The Day when there will not benefit [anyone] wealth or children. But only one who comes to Allāh with a sound heart" (al-Shu'ara 26:88-89).

And so, to guide mankind to their own salvation, the Prophet ﷺ was sent to purify the hearts of mankind through spiritual exercise and reform their behavior by way of divine law. This was the basis of his mission as Allāh states what means, "It is He who has sent among the unlettered, a Messenger from themselves reciting to them His verses and purifying them and teaching them the Book and wisdom, although they were before in clear error" (al-Jumu'ah 62:2).

Over the centuries, our revered scholars have exerted all efforts to document and canonize that process to preserve it for future generations. While the Islamic law has been preserved in the legal manuals of master jurists, the science of spiritual growth and development has been captured by the works and practices of Ṣufi masters.

One such work is the <u>Inauguration of the Jurist and Linguist into the Gardens of Love and Gnosis</u> by Imām al-Wāsiṭī. This work serves as a foundational treatise in spirituality and is now in your hands, translated and published in the English language for the first time.

This translation project was undertaken in the month of Ramaḍān, a month of inward reflection and purification. The aim was to provide the English-speaking Muslim with a foundation upon which to build their spiritual pursuits, guiding them to a balanced and orthodox approach.

Along with the translation, a rather succinct series of videos was recorded to provide the reader with further clarification and examples of contemporary application of al-Wasiṭī's principles. In the process of recording the videos, which are available online, the rough draft of this translation was shared with a hand full of seekers who provided insightful feedback and suggestions.

A debt of gratitude is owed to Ḥasan Ṣiddiqui who assisted in reviewing and editing the entire text. Warm words of appreciation are also extended to our new-found friend and brother along the journey, Dr. Arjan Post who was gracious enough to increase the value of this work with a brief biography of the author. His doctoral research on the Imām, Ibn Shaykh al-Ḥazzamiyīn, is priceless and his suggestions and conversations during the translation process were greatly appreciated. May Allāh reward all of them!

Fraternally,

John Starling

About the Author

He is ʿImād al-Dīn Aḥmad b. Ibrāhīm b. ʿAbd al-Raḥmān b. Masʿūd b. ʿUmar Abū al-ʿAbbās al-Wāsiṭī al-Ḥazzāmī al-Dimashqī – may Allāh sanctify his spirit. He was also known under the nickname '*Ibn shaykh al-Ḥazzāmiyyīn*,' which may be rendered as 'son of the shaykh of the Ḥazzāmites,' referring to the fact that his father was a spiritual master of the Rifāʿiyya Sufi order for inhabitants of the Ḥazzāmī quarter in Wāsiṭ.

In 657/1259 al-Wāsiṭī was born in this city, where he would also spend his youth and begin his studies in the religious sciences. Although it no longer exists today, it was once located in Southern Iraq, just above the marshlands (*al-baṭā'iḥ*) from whence Aḥmad al-Rifāʿī, the founder of the Rifāʿiyya, hailed. Al-Wāsiṭī's father was Shāfiʿī, so he himself naturally grew up following the same *madhhab*. It is likely that he also received some instruction in the Ashʿarī school of theology, as he mentions in several of his works that his teachers in Shāfiʿī jurisprudence were Ashʿarīs. As a child, his father exposed him to the rituals of the Rifāʿī Sufis, which he would gradually come to dislike more and more. He began reading the books of the Sufis on his own, such as the *Risāla* of al-Qushayrī, the *Qūt al-Qulūb* of Abū Ṭālib al-Makkī, and the *Iḥyā'* of al-Ghazālī. He came to the conclusion that the practices of the Rifāʿiyya did not reflect the spirit of Sufism he found in these books. At some point he decided to focus instead on the study of Shāfiʿī *fiqh*, as he realized that knowledge of Sharīʿa was imperative to a sound spiritual state. While he was pleased to become acquainted with Allāh's rulings, he was disappointed in the fact that his Shāfiʿī teachers seemed to completely disregard the inner dimension of Islam, so that *fiqh* had become nothing more than an academic discipline to them.

At some point he went to Baghdad to continue his studies in jurisprudence. Since Iraq's capital was famed for its Sufi tradition, it is not surprising that he came to accompany a group of Sufis there as well. He found that the Baghdadi Sufis had much greater regard for the revealed law than the Rifāʿiyya and was thus pleased to find a more grounded spirituality among them. However, like the Rifāʿīs, they too practiced the ritual known as *samāʿ* (Sufi audition). This usually involved the chanting of poems to a certain rhythm, to which some Sufis would perform a spiritual dance (*raqṣ*). From al-Wasiti's viewpoint, this practice had no basis in the Sharīʿa and was thus a blameworthy innovation (*bidʿa*) that ought to be censured.

After some time, he performed the greater pilgrimage (*ḥajj*) in Makkah al-Mukarrama, where he is related to have also sat with a group of Shāfiʿī scholars.

Somewhere during the last fifteen years of the seventh/thirteenth century, he set out again to continue his search for spiritual guidance. This took him to Egypt, where he first stayed in Alexandria and later moved to Cairo. In Alexandria he accompanied the Shādhiliyya, and it was this Sufi order that would have the greatest impact on his outlook on Sufism. Many important principles of his own Sufi teachings are in fact grounded in Shādhilī Sufism. His shaykh in the order was the Persian Shāfiʿī Najm al-Dīn ʿAbd Allāh al-Iṣbahānī (d. 721/1321), a rather obscure figure today, but clearly a renowned spiritual mentor during these days, and definitely in the eyes of al-Wāsiṭī. For our Iraqi spiritual seeker, the Shādhilīs were unique in their time: their Sufism was practical and deeply concerned with upholding the rulings of the Sharīʿa. At the same time, they were critical of other Sufis who would fail to practice Sufism within the boundaries set by Allāh, and, as such, did not practice *samāʿ*, for instance. Although this initially seemed like the end of his journey, al-Wāsiṭī had by then become aware of the theological teachings of the scholars from the Ahl al-Ḥadīth, which had made him quite critical of rational *kalām*-theology, and thus of Ashʿarism – and the followers of the Shādhiliyya were all Ashʿarīs. This appears to have been his main motivation to eventually leave the Sufi order and move to Cairo, though he clearly remained indebted to them – a fact he does not deny in his books.

In Cairo he lived in several Sufi convents (*khānqāh*s), which were madrasa-like buildings that offered housing to wandering Sufis and served as a platform for them to practice Sufism communally and study the religious sciences. Such convents were often sponsored by Mamluk officials, and had by then become a widely accepted part of the religious landscape. Al-Wāsiṭī was not impressed by the life in the convents, as he felt that Sufism there had become completely degraded to the degree that it was nothing more than a set of conventions that were to be followed, so that one was to appear as a Sufi on the outside only. However, the true purpose of Sufism, to arrive unto Allāh spiritually and attain His lofty friendship, was not truly sought out. And even worse, he found that the Sufis in the convents were quite receptive to the monistic teachings of Muḥyī al-Dīn Ibn ʿArabī (d. 638/1240). When he began to understand what these teachings actually entail, he fell into something of a spiritual depression and left Egypt for good. Later on, in Damascus he would compose several refutations against Ibn ʿArabī and his school of Sufism.

Just before the turn of the eighth/fourteenth century he arrived in Damascus, which in a sense had by then become the new capital of Ḥanbalism. Many renowned Ḥanbalī families from around the Muslim world had settled there, some fleeing from the crusades, others from the Mongol invasion. Al-Wāsiṭī became greatly impressed with the piety and religiosity of the Ḥanbalīs and finally decided to convert to their *madhhab*, perhaps under the guidance of the shaykh al-Islām Taqī al-Dīn Aḥmad Ibn Taymiyya (d. 728/1328). In any case, he did soon recognize Ibn Taymiyya as the greatest shaykh of his age and joined his inner-circle of associates, friends, and pupils. He began studying Ḥanbalī *fiqh*, the *sīra* of the Prophet (saw), and Ahl al-Ḥadīth theology.

He spent the last ten years of his life formulating Sufi teachings that were in accordance with the principles and religiosity of the

Ḥanbalīs and the Ahl al-Ḥadīth, and taught these to his disciples and friends in Damascus. Among them were several members of Ibn Taymiyya's inner-circle, such as Shams al-Dīn Muḥammad al-Dhahabī (d. 748/1348), Zayn al-Dīn ʿAbd al-Raḥmān al-Baʿlabakkī (d. 734/1333), Ibrāhīm al-Qawwās al-Dimashqī (d. 761/1360), and Ibn Qayyim al-Jawziyya (d. 751/1350). Ibn Taymiyya is known to have greatly respected al-Wāsiṭī as a Sufi master. He viewed him as one of the rare Sufis of his day who still walked in the footsteps of the Sufi shaykhs of old, the shaykhs Ibn Taymiyya himself also revered as gnostics (*ʿārifīn*). This is exemplified above all by the fact that he would refer to al-Wāsiṭī as "the Junayd of his time."[1]

In his Damascene days our Iraqi Sufi master composed many writings in the field of Sufism, several works on the life of the Prophet (saw), and some theological treatises.[2] Among his Sufi writings the book that is now before you, *Madkhal ahl al-fiqh wa-al-lisān ilā maydān al-maḥabba wa-al-ʿirfān*, is one of the most comprehensive and representative of his vision of Sufism.

Al-Wāsiṭī passed away in 711/1311 in the small hospital of the old city of Damascus. He was buried on the slopes of Mount Qāsyūn – a blessed resting place indeed, amidst many Ḥanbalī brethren who had gone before him. May Allāh have mercy on them all and grant them Jannah!

---

[1] Abū al-Qāsim al-Junayd (d. 297/910) was a Baghdadi Sufi master who is widely regarded as "the master of the Sufi community" (*sayyid al-ṭāʾifa*). Sunni scholars often refer to his teachings as representative of orthodox Sufism, and Ibn Taymiyya certainly views them as such in his own writings on Sufism.

[2] For a list of al-Wāsiṭī's writings see the first section in the bibliography of: Post, *The Journeys of a Taymiyyan Sufi*.

Introduction

In the name of Allāh the Most Merciful the Most Beneficent. We seek His aid and send salutations of prayer and peace upon the master Muḥammad, his family, and all his companions.

The Shaykh, Imām, scholar, one-of-a-kind, inquisitor, ʿImād al-Dīn Aḥmad b. Ibrāhīm al-Wāsiṭī, may Allāh perpetuate his lofty status and exalted mention, stated the following:

All praise belongs to Allāh Who has revealed the way of guidance and reason, saved those He loves from alienation, removed the shrouded cloak of anxiety with the path of truth, benefited those who, in repentance, have returned to His pleasure, Who has cultivated them through the ascending levels of deeds and character in order to obtain the objective, Who has purified them from the tarnish of dark and murky human nature, thus completely preparing them for an inundation of light, Who weaned them from sin and nourished them with righteousness, and thus they wholeheartedly directed themselves to Him whereas before they were severely astray.

He has removed the veil from their hearts and shown them the statutes of mutual intimacy, thus their hearts, through love and friendship, were drawn to love like steel is to a magnet, eternally enlivening their hearts, connecting with Him in an everlasting inseparable manner. He roused, taught, and refined them and so, after blindness, they opened their eyes of insightfulness to Him, fixating their gaze without control while their hearts wandered in the open plains of divine proximity after they were imprisoned in the straits of existence, deteriorating along the descending rungs of contradiction.

بسم الله الرحمن الرحيم وبه نستعين

والصلاة والسلام على سيدنا محمد وآله وصحبه أجمعين.

قال الشيخ الإمام العلامة الفريد المحقق عماد الدين أحمد بن إبراهيم الواسطي أدام الله علو قدره وسمو ذكره.

الحمد لله الذي فتح مناهج الهدى والرشاد لمن أحبه فأنقذه من الإبعاد وخلع العناية المحفوفة بالسداد على المنيبين إلى رضاه وأفاد وهذبهم في مدارج الأعمال والأخلاق لنيل المراد وصفاهم من كدر الطباع البشرية ذات الظلمات والسواد ليستعدوا بذلك لفيض الأنوار بكمال التأهب والاستعداد فطمهم عن المخالفات وغذاهم بالموافقات فأقبلوا بوجوه قلوبهم عليه وكانوا قبل ذلك من الشراد.

كشف لقلوبهم الحجاب وأراهم لوائح الاقتراب فانجذبت قلوبهم إلى المحبة انجذاب الحديد إلى المغناطيس بالمحبة والوداد حييت به قلوبهم الحياة الأبدية واتصلت به اتصالا لا انفصام له أبد الآباد أيقظهم وعلمهم وهذبهم ففتحوا عيون بصائرهم إليه بعد العمى وحفوا به بلا استبداد جالت قلوبهم في فضاء القرب بعد سجنهم في مضائق الأكوان وترديها في دركات الأضداد.

With their hearts, they have departed from this world to the Hereafter, seeking residence with their beloved in the land of servitude—the best resting place—which in the presence of the All-Powerful rumbles like a roaring kettle, boiling with love, exaltation, reverence, utter destitution, and in need of support, all the while receiving from Him increased connection with innumerable epiphanies and various wonders. They witness with their hearts what eyes cannot see. In Him they take delight, from Him they are fearful, and to Him they are devoted; both the seeker (*murīd*) and the sought after (*murād*).

I bear witness that there is no deity worthy of worship other than Allāh, alone and without partner, the sustainer maintaining His servants, who includes them in His bounty and ever-increasing favor.

I bear witness that Muḥammad ﷺ is His servant and messenger, the originator of good, the medium to all favor whose return is awaited in the Hereafter. May prayers be upon him, his family, and companions so long as his virtue is sought by the arrivers and the people of love emanate because of divine nexus.

If Allāh were to open the servant's insight into the various sciences and provide him with a clear mind and a window into comprehension who nurses from the legal sciences a full term, comes into possession, from its raiment, of a beautiful veil, effectively contemplates on the details of commands and prohibitions, is aware of the manner in which incidents are attributed to the source origins, then he will be worthy of donning the cloak of their deeds and to taste the pure of their spirits and the realities of their states. This is what the soundness of the servant is based on, because the servant's full integrity is only reached through sound servitude of Allāh ﷻ which is made up of an outer body, an inclined spirit (*nafs*), a distinguished mind, a governing heart, and an integral soul (*rūḥ*).

خرجوا من الدنيا إلى الآخرة بقلوبهم فتوطنوا هناك بين يدي محبوبهم أوطان العبودية على أحسن المهاد فلها في حضرة العزيز أزيز كأزيز المراجل من غليانها بالمحبة والتعظيم والخشية والافتقار والاسترفاد ولهم منه على مدد الأوقات تزايد الصلات من منح الجليات وأنواع الكرامات ما يعجز عن حصره العباد يرون بقلوبهم ما غاب عن العيان فبه يلتذون ومنه يخافون وعليه يعكفون فمنهم المريد والمراد.

وأشهد أن لا إله إلا الله وحده لا شريك له القائم بقيوميته على العباد الشامل لهم بكرمه وفضله المستزاد.

وأشهد أن محمدا ﷺ عبده ورسوله فاتح الخير والواسطة إلى كل فضل تنتظر عائدته في المعاد صلوات الله عليه وعلى آله وأصحابه ما قام على باب فضله الوراد وصدر بجوائز الصلات أهل الوداد وبعد.

فإن العبد إذا فتح الله بصيرته في فنون العلوم وأمده بصفاء العقل ونوافذ الفهوم وارتضع من العلوم الشرعية أكمل الرضاع وصار له من كسوتها أحسن القناع ونفذ فكره في تفاصيل الأمر والنهي وعرف طريق رد الحوادث إلى الأصول فحقيق به أن يكتسي ملابس أعمالها ويذوق رائق أشربتها وحقائق أحوالها فكمال العبد متوقف على ذلك لأن كمال العبد إنما يتم بكمال عبوديته لله عز وجل وهو مركب من جسم ظاهر ونفس مائلة وعقل مميز وقلب حاكم وروح كلية.

The pinnacle of bodily servitude is proficiently performing actions of the law and refraining from its prohibitions with clarity and comprehension.

The pinnacle of the spirit's servitude is in its alignment with its Master, loving what He loves and despising what He despises. This only holds true for those with a tranquil soul and not for those with an inciting or blameworthy soul.

The pinnacle of intellectual servitude is in filling it with the intricacies of the knowledge of commands and prohibitions, its adept insight into that knowledge, and its skillful and sound acumen.

The pinnacle of the heart's servitude is the dedication of its focus to the divine attributes, establishing the rulings of their devotion such as fear and hope, reverential fear and pleasure, trust, general love, divine supervision, etc, which pertain to the servitude derived from the rulings of the divine attributes.

The pinnacle of the soul's servitude is its release into the open plains of divine proximity, its passion for exclusive love which sets it ablaze via the traces of The Owner of Majesty and Honor which are revealed to it. It thus becomes a rolling sea from the breezes of divine proximity and winds of sincere affection, ignited by the fires of love, and captivated by the gravitational forces of yearning.

Whoever seeks to perfect their disposition (*firṭah*) and desires to rectify their nature (*jibillah*) must seek to perfect every part, the body, the spirit, the mind, the heart, and the soul and beware of leaving this world while a part of you is deficient and has not served Allāh ﷻ in its associated manner of worship. If you are incapable of perfecting every part of your being, as has been explained, then you must believe in it and be aware of it, for whoever knows something and believes in it, even though they are unable to obtain it, has risen above the peculiars of ignorance.

فكمال عبودية الجسم القيام بأعمال الشرع واجتنابه مناهيه وإتقان ذلك العمل والاجتناب بالتصفية والاستيعاب.

وكمال عبودية النفس موافقة مولاها في محبة ما أحبه وكراهية ما كرهه وهذا إنما يصح لأهل النفوس المطمئنة ويتعذر على أهل النفوس الأمارة واللوامة.

وكمال عبودية العقل امتلاؤه بتفاصيل علوم الأمر والنهي وحذاقة البصيرة فيه مع المهارة وحسن التبصر.

وكمال عبودية القلب افتتاح بصره في الصفات والقيام بأحكام عبودياتها من الخوف الرجاء والخشية والرضا والتوكل والمحبة العامة والمراقبة وغير ذلك من العبوديات المقتضية لأحكام الصفات.

وكمال عبودية الروح انطلاقها في فضاء القرب ووجدانها للحب الخاص الملهب لها بواسطة ما يبدو عليها من آثار الجلال والإكرام فتصير بحرا مواجا من نسيم القرب وروح الأنس ملتهبة بنيران الحب مجذوبة بجواذب الشوق.

فيا من يطلب تكميل فطرته ويروم إصلاح جبلته عليك بطلب الكمال لكل جزء منك من جسمك ونفسك وعقلك وقلبك وروحك واحذر أن تخرج من الدنيا وبعض من أبعاضك ناقص لم يقم لله عز جل بما تعبده به فإن عجزت عن تكميل كل جزء منك بما قد شرح فكن بذلك مؤمنا وبه عالما فمن علم شيئا وآمن به ارتقى بذلك عن خصوص الجهل به مع التخلف عن نيله

Your rising above the depths of ignorance to knowledge is more tolerable than the degradation of both ignorance and neglect. One evil is more tolerable than two, one loss is better than two and it is Allāh with whom help is sought.

So long as you have understood that, put faith in it, and become aware of the virtue of someone of integrity, the severe need for it should be clear to you and you will have become aware of the spiritual guides' virtue, the realized virtue of following their judgement, yielding to them and being well-mannered with them. You will have also become aware of the true loss due to missing out on their companionship, not benefiting from them, opposing them, and poor compliance with them.

So, maintain manners with them like the experienced seekers and protect them for the sake of Allāh. Look to them for the first and the last, the hidden and the apparent and do not attach your heart to them without Allāh and, God willing, Allāh will preserve your integrity by way of them.

Etiquette of accompanying the teachers is given precedence over all etiquettes; whoever preserves it, Allāh will preserve their state of being in relation to their etiquette with them. Such a transaction with Allāh includes politely listening to them, abandoning any discord with them, forgoing any accusations against them or argumentation with them, politely seeking clarification, with gentle words, for their ambiguous expressions or inner-states (*ḥāl/awḥāl*), to be kind and humble with them, to be quiet when they are in a state of contraction (*qabḍ*), to take advantage of the time when they are in a state of expansion (*basṭ*), and to be in need of Allāh ﷻ regarding it all in order that the servants care be entrusted to Him. They are the intermediaries, from their manners, the provisions of the path are obtained, and from their robes, the light of the quest is perceived.

فارتقاؤك من درك الجهل إلى العلم به أهون من الانحطاط في الجهل مع القصور فشر واحد أهون من شرين وفوت واحد أقرب من فوتين وبالله المستعان.

إذا علمت ذلك وآمنت به وعرفت فضل صاحب الكمال تبين لك شدة الافتقار إلى ذلك وعرفت فضل المرشدين إلى ذلك والفضل الحاصل بتحكيمهم والانقياد لهم والأدب معهم وعرفت النقص الواقع بفوات صحبتهم وعدم الانتفاع بهم وبمخالفتهم بسوء التأتي معهم.

فتأدب معهم بآداب الطلبة الأكياس واحفظهم وعامل الله تعالى بذلك وانظر إليه في الأول والآخر والظاهر والباطن ولا تعلق قلبك بهم دون الله يحفظ الله عز وجل عليك كمالك إن شاء الله تعالى بهم.

فأدب صحبة الأستاذين مقدم على كل أدب من حفظه حفظ الله عليه حاله بحسب أدبه معهم ومعاملة الله عز وجل بذلك من حسن الإصغاء إليهم وترك الخلاف عليهم وترك اتهامهم والمماراة لهم وحسن الاستكشاف لما يشكل من عباراتهم وأحوالهم بلطيف الكلام وخفض الجناح لهم والسكوت عند قبضهم واغتنام أوقات بسطهم والافتقار إلى الله عز جل في ذلك كله ليتولى حفظ العبد فيه فهؤلاء هم الوسائط تستفاد أحكام الطريق من أدبهم وتستشف من ردائهم أنوار المطلوب.

Manners with them are considered manners with Allāh ﷻ and His messenger ﷺ because they are his inheritors, they have inherited a portion of his inner-state just as the jurist has inherited a portion of his outer action, and all are contributors to the endeavor. Success lies with Allāh.

Origins of Gnosis and Love of Allāh

The foundation of gnosis is faith in Allāh, the Mighty and Majestic, and His messenger ﷺ. Faith emerges from awareness of the messenger ﷺ by knowing his biography, sunnah, battles, miracles, signs, and wonders. Based on that, the significance of prophethood becomes known and its proofs and evidence emerge in the heart.

When the significance of prophethood is known and its signs and evidence are settled in the hearts, it becomes a seat for the knowledge of monotheism (*tawḥīd*) and a path to gnosis of the Magnificent Lord who sent and dispatched them. This is because prophethood is from the signs, proofs, and evidence of Allāh ﷻ for those with the capacity to understand and are free of turbidity and seek to be rid of it.

Most of those who have been veiled from the realities of monotheism, even though they are knowledgeable of the sunnah and its intricacies, have been veiled because they simply sought the legal rulings from the sunnah and their aspirations did not include awareness of faith's realities. If they were to intentionally seek it, they would have understood, but their aspirations were directed to the love of this world and the obtainment of lofty positions within it. Their hearts have opened to the auspices of this world, turned away from the auspices of the Hereafter, and are concealed from the proof of gnosis and relish of love. They did not surpass the outward appearance of the divine law and rulings to the realities of their inner-dimensions and their significance in reference to divine gnosis and so the light of the divine attributes and the knowledge of divine action radiated not in their hearts.

فالأدب معهم هو من الأدب مع الله عز وجل ومع رسوله ﷺ لأنهم ورثته ورثوا قسطا من حاله الباطن كما ورث الفقهاء قسطا من علمه الظاهر والكل مشتركون في العمل وبالله التوفيق.

فصل في بيان منشأ المعرفة والمحبة لله عز وجل من أين تنشأ ومن ماذا تنشأ

أصل المعرفة الإيمان بالله عز وجل وبرسوله ﷺ بمعرفة سيرته وسنته وغزواته ومعجزاته وآياته وكراماته فبذلك يعلم شأن النبوة وتلوح أدلتها وبراهينها في القلوب.

ومتى علم شأن النبوة ورسخت معالمها ودلائلها في القلوب كانت كرسيا لعلم التوحيد وطريقا إلى معرفة الرب العظيم المرسل الباعث لأن النبوة آيات الله عز وجل وبيناته ودلالاته لمن اتسع فهمه وصفا من الكدر وطلب استخراج ذلك منه.

وإنما حجب أكثر من حجب عن حقائق علم التوحيد وإن كانوا عالمين بالسنة وتفاصيلها لأنهم يطلبون من السنة معرفة الأحكام وهممهم قاصرة عن طلب السنة لمعرفة حقائق الإيمان ولو طلبوه مع المشيئة لأدركوه فهممهم منصرفة إلى محبة الدنيا ومناصبها والرفعة فيها قد سرحت قلوبهم في أكناف الدنيا وانصرفت عن أكناف الآخرة وحجبت عن شهود المعرفة وذوق المحبة ولم يتجاوزوا صورة الشريعة وظهواهر الأحكام إلى حقائق أسرارها مدلولاتها من المعارف الإلهية فلم يشرق في قلوبهم شيء من أنوار الصفات ولا معارف الأفعال.

Whoever desires gnosis of Allāh ﷻ, whose spirit has turned away from the world and its desires, and makes their path to its obtainment the Book of Allāh and sunnah of His Messenger ﷺ, will ascend from the outward sunnah to its inner-dimensions, if desired, with the supervision of the teachers who act as portals to it, and have the light of the Book and sunnah radiate in the hearts of its sincere seekers.

It is the light hidden within the legal code and rulings, which acts as a veil for that light, not to be removed except for the heart of one who believes Allāh in his quest and in seeking His gnosis and love, resulting, by the will of Allāh ﷻ, in its rending. Whoever renders it, faith will enter their pure heart and they will come to know the Mighty and Majestic Lord, who sent the prophets with His legal code and rulings, by His names, attributes, and actions. The effects of those names and attributes will emerge in the hearts after knowledge of the rulings and legal code is obtained and taken as a habitual adornment, and thus their light will emanate in that heart which is pleased and purified from the love of this world and position, abstains from it, desires the Hereafter and what resides with Allāh, and loves divine gnosis and heavenly experiences.

It is well known that the veil which conceals that is nothing more than devoting one's aspirations to the world, desiring it, and turning away from the love of Allāh ﷻ and divine proximity. And that, the path to its attainment, coupled with asceticism, is the Book of Allāh the Mighty and Majestic and the sunnah of His messenger ﷺ with the teachers' supervision as previously mentioned.

ومن أحب معرفة الله عز وجل وعزفت نفسه عن الدنيا وشهواتها وجعل طريقه إلى ذلك كتاب الله وسنة رسول الله ﷺ ترقى من ظاهر السنة إلى باطنها بتوقيف الأستاذين النافذين إلى ذلك مع المشيئة فانبثق في قلوب الصادقين الطالبين لذلك أنوار المعارف من الكتاب والسنة.

وهو النور المستجن في ضمن الشرائع والأحكام فالشارئع والأحكام هو كالستر على ذلك النور لا يكشف ذلك الستر إلا عن قلب من صدق الله في طلبه معرفته ومحبته فيخرقه حينئذ بمشيئة الله عز وجل فمن خرقه باشر الإيمان صفو قلبه وعرف الرب عز وجل الباعث للأنبياء بشرائعه وأحكامه بأسمائه وصفاته وأفعاله فتلوح آثار الأسماء والصفات في القلوب بعد معرفة الأحكام والشرائع والتلبس بها فتلوح أنوارها في ذلك القلب المرتاض المطهر من حب الدنيا والمناصب الزاهد فيها الراغب في الآخرة وفيما عند الله المحب للمعارف الإلـهية والأذواق القدسية.

فقد عرفت أن الحجاب عن ذلك إنما هو انصراف الهمم إلى الدنيا والرغبة فيها وإعراضها عن محبة الله عز وجل وطلبه والقرب منه وأن الطريق إلى حصول ذلك مع الزهد كتاب الله عز وجل وسنة رسوله ﷺ بتوقيف الأستاذين كما تقدم.

The Principles of this Pursuit's Maxims

Principle One: Authentic Revealed Doctrine

It is stipulated to have faith in all of that as intended by Allāh ﷻ and His messenger ﷺ, comprehending it as this nation's predecessors did such as the traditionists (*Ahl al-Ḥadīth*) the likes of Aḥmad, his disciples, contemporaries, and peers; like the great Imām al-Shāfʿī, Mālik, Abū Ḥanīfah ﵃ and their followers, while remaining distant from the speculative and rationalist theologians (*Ahl al-Kalam wa al-Naẓr*). The companions ﵃ did not adopt the religion of Allāh ﷻ which He revealed to His messenger ﷺ, except by way of pure faith, belief, and acceptance. They did not need to be aware of it nor did they need to learn about the implicate and the implicant (*al-lāzim wa al-malzūm*) and the like.

We have certainly witnessed those who are skilled in rationalist theology, while their adversary representing the truth was of a lesser degree, be able turn the realities upside down, making falsehood appear as the truth and the truth as falsehood, due to them being more eloquent in their argument than their adversary who possesses the truth.

We are therefore sufficed by the way of our original predecessors, finding adequacy in what was adequate for them in all things; who were the companions, those that followed, and those that then proceeded the followers in righteousness ﵃ along with the path of our shaykhs in this school such as al-Junayd and his contemporaries and those who came later such as Shaykh al-Islām ʿAbdullāh al-Anṣāri al-Harawi and Shaykh ʿAbd al-Qādir al-Jīlī ﵃.

Doctrines are the foundations upon which spectacles (*mashāhid*) are built and spectacles are the foundation of seats (*maqāʿid*). Whoever's doctrine is sound, so too will be his spectacle and his seat will ascend to the highest levels. Whosoever's doctrine is corrupted, so too will be his spectacle and his seat will descend to the lowest levels.

فصل في بيان الأصول التي عليها تبتنى قواعد هذا الشأن

الأصل الأول صحة الاعتقاد في جميع ما جاء عن الله عز وجل وعن رسول ﷺ

فيشترط له الإيمان بجميع ذلك على مراد الله عز وجل ومراد رسول الله ﷺ وليفهم من ذلك ما فهمه سلف الأمة من أهل الحديث كأحمد وأصحابه وأقرانهم ونظرائهم وكالأمام الأعظم الشافعي ومالك وأبي حنيفة رضي الله عنهم وأتباعهم مع البعد عن أهل الكلام والنظر فأن الصحابة رضي الله عنهم لم يأخذوا دين الله عز وجل الذي أنزله على رسوله ﷺ إلا بمجرد الإيمان والتصديق والقبول فلم يفتقروا في معرفته وتلقيه إلى معرفة اللازم والملزوم وغير ذلك.

وقد رأينا من يكون حاذقا بالنظر وخصمه في الحق دونه في ذلك يقلب بحذاقته بالنظر الحقائق فيجعل الباطل حقا والحق باطلا لكونه ألحن بحجته من خصمه صاحب الحق.

فيكفينا في ذلك طريقة سلفنا الأولين ليسعنا ما وسعهم في كل شيء وهم الصحابة والتابعون وتابعوهم بإحسان رضي الله عنهم وطريقة شيوخنا في هذا المذهب كالجنيد وأقرانه ومن جاء بعدها كشيخ الإسلام عند الله الأنصاري الهروي والشيخ الإمام عبد القادر الجيلي رضي الله عنهم أجمعين.

فالعقائد أصول المشاهد عليها تبتنى والمشاهد أصول المقاعد فمن صح معتقده صح مشهده وارتقى إلى الدرجات العالية مقعده ومن فسد معتقده فسد مشهده وانحط إلى الدركات السفلى مقعده.

You must know that faith in the doctrine of divine loftiness and highness (*al-ʿulū wa al-fawqiyyah*)—without comprehension, defining modality or limitation, assigning likeness, quiddity, or comparison, just as it has been mentioned in the Mighty Book and authentic sunnah—is at the foundation of this topic and serves as its base.

Whoever is well-versed in this issue of doctrine will, in their heart, find a qiblah to their Master and Maker, utilized when turning to Him, praying to Him, worshiping Him, and for all their other endeavors, be they apparent or hidden, becoming a point of attachment for their heart, which wanders about into other things, eventually returning to the point of its connection just as the steed wanders only to return to their hitching post.

واعلم أن الإيمان بمسألة العلو والفوقية من غير إحاطة ولا كيفية ولا حصر ولا تمثيل ولا تشبيه كما ورد ذلك في الكتاب العزيز وفي السنة الصحيحة هو أصل هذا الشأن وأساسه.

فمن رسخ في هذه المسألة صار لقلبه قبلة إلى مولاه وفاطره في توجهه وصلاته وعبادته وسائر مساعيه الظاهرة والباطنة وصار ذلك لقلبه معلقا يجول قلبه في الأشياء ثم يعود إلى معلقه كالفرس يجول ثم يعود إلى أخيته.

Principle Two: Awakening

Awakening (*yaqaẓah*) is the foundation of the virtuous stations (*maqāmāt*) and lofty states (*aḥwāl*). It is essentially the awakening of the heart from the slumber of heedlessness and preparation for the meeting with Allāh ﷻ. Allāh ﷻ said, "[It will be said], 'You were certainly in heedlessness of this, and We have removed from you your cover, so your sight, this Day, is sharp.'"

That which veils the servant from rectifying their state (*ḥāl*) and preparing for The Return includes: high expectations, love of the immediate and preference of it over the distant which results in the servants blindness to what is awaiting them such as the various stages of death, the grave, and the Hereafter.

If Allāh desires good for one of His servants, He awakens their heart from the slumber of heedlessness and brings death to their attention. He then progresses their heart through the stations of the Hereafter, station by station, level by level, and thus they ponder over the sudden rush of death which leads to their preparedness for what is in front of them so that they can meet their Lord ﷻ with a radiant face. It is indeed possible that the servant falls ill for a few days and is transported to Allāh ﷻ before rectifying their state, resulting in extensive regret and an inability to make up for what was lost.

The wise are those who do not wake nor sleep except having committed deeds with which they are pleased to meet Allāh ﷻ. The negligent are those who delay repentance to the morrow and beyond.

If the servant is able, they should be mindful of death and its immediacy and the grave and their isolation in it, accompanied by nothing but their deeds, both their righteous and wicked deeds, which will join them in the grave just as has been reported in the ḥadith narrated by al-Barāʾ b. ʿĀzib and Abū Hurayrah,

الأصل الثاني اليقظة

اليقظة هي أصل المقامات الشريفة والأحوال العالية وهي عبارة عن انتباه القلب عن رقدة الغفلات والاستعداد للقاء الله عز وجل. قال الله عز وجل ﴿لقد كنت في غفلة من هذا فكشفنا عنك غطاءك فبصرك اليوم حديد﴾.

وإنما يحجب العبد عن إصلاح الحال والاستعداد للمآل طول الأمل وحب العاجلة وإيثارها على الآجلة فيعمى بذلك العبد عن ما بين يديه من أمور الموت والبرزخ والآخرة.

فإذا أراد الله بعبد خيرا أيقظ قلبه من سنة الغفلة وأحضر الموت بين يديه وسار بقلبه في مقامات الآخرة ومواقفها مقاما مقاما ومنزلا منزلا ففكر في هجوم الأجل على بغتة فاستعد حينئذ لما بين يديه ليلقى ربه عز وجل في الآخرة بوجه أبيض فإن العبد ربما مرض أياما يسيرة وانتقل إلى الله عز وجل قبل إصلاح الحال فيطول لذلك ندمه ويعجز عن استدراك ما فاته.

فالعاقل هو الذي لا يصبح ولا يمسي إلا على عمل يحب لقاء الله عز وجل عليه والمفرط هو المسوف والتوبة من اليوم إلى غد ومن غد إلى بعد غد.

فالعبد إذا استحضر الموت وهجومه والقبر والانفرادة فيه بأعماله فيلحقه في القبر نعيم الأعمال الصالحة وعقوبات الأعمال الطالحة كما في الحديث

"Surely, the righteous servant, when placed in their grave, will be asked; a caller will call from the heavens, 'My servant has spoken the truth so make bedding for him from Paradise, clothe him from Paradise, and open a door of Paradise for him' and its breeze and fragrance will come to him. As for the disbeliever, a caller will call out from the heavens, 'My servant has concealed it, so make for him bedding from the fire, clothe him from the fire, and open a door from the fire for him' and its heat and scorching fire will come to him".

Likewise, the servant will remember the Day of Resurrection and their standing before Allāh ﷻ, being driven, barefoot, naked, hungry, and thirsty to the Maḥshar with the driver and the witness to stand at that extensive site for 50,000 years.

The sun will be in proximity to the peoples' heads according to their deeds, the books will be dispersed and there will be those who take their book in their right hand while others will take their book behind the back.

Then comes The Reckoning. Each servant will be measured regarding their life and how they led it; their youth, how they used it; and their wealth, how they earned it and how they spent it.

The scales will then be erected, the records will be opened, and the crossing of the slippery stumble-inducing bridge will occur, along with the various other sites awaiting us.

If the servant is able to ponder, with certainty, over them, knowing that there is no salvation except by the grace of Allāh and the rectification of their actions in this world, it will all serve as a catalyst requiring an awakening and an attentiveness from the deluge of heedlessness, preparedness for the Hereafter through rectification of state, and abandonment of negligence and carelessness. And so, while fearing the rush of death while negligent and heedless before preparations have been made,

إن العبد الصالح إذا وضع في قبره وسئل نادى مناد من السماء أن صدق عبدي فأفرشوه من الجنة وألبسوه من الجنة وافتحوا له بابا إلى الجنة قال فيأتيه من روحها وطيبها. وأما الكافر فينادي مناد من السماء أن كذب عبدي فأفرشوه من النار وألبسوه من النار وافتحوا له بابا إلى النار فيأتي من حرها وسمومها رواه البراء بن عازب وأبو هريرة في المسانيد.

وكذلك يستحضر العبد يوم القيامة ووقوفه بين يدي الله عز وجل وسياقته إلى المحشر مع السائق والشهيد حافيا عاريا جائعا ظمآن فيقف في ذلك الموقف الطويل خمسين ألف سنة.

وتدنو الشمس من رؤوس الخلائق على قدر أعمالهم وتطاير الكتب فآخذ كتابه بيمينه وآخذ كتابه من وراء ظهره.

ثم الحساب فيحاسب العبد عن عمره فيما أفناه وعن شبابه فيما أبلاه وعن ماله من أين اكتسبه وفيما أنفقه.

ثم نصب الموازين ونشر الدواوين والعبور على الصراط الدحض المزلة وغير ذلك من المواقف التي بين أيدينا.

فإذا فكر العبد فيها موقنا بها عالما أنه لا ينجيه في ذلك اليوم إلا رحمة الله وإصلاحه لأعماله في الدنيا كان ذلك كله مما يوجب اليقظة والانتباه من غمار الغفلة والاستعداد للآخرة بإصلاح الحال وترك التفريط والإهمال خشية هجوم الآجال على غرة غفلة قبل الاستعداد

they will conclude that day as residents of the grave in the encampment of the deceased unable to increase in good deeds or remove a single sin.

On that subject, the Prophet ﷺ said, "Increase in the remembrance of that which severs pleasure for it is not remembered often except that it disparages him".

If the servant awakens while in good health, free, and young, they can make up for what they missed, and eliminate the consequences.

A ḥadīth regarding this states, "Two blessings which are spoiled by many people; health and free time".

Also, "Take advantage of five before five; your youth before your old age, your health before you are sick, your life before your death, your free time before you are busy, and your time in this world before you are in the Hereafter".

For tomorrow, you will not even know your own name.

فيمسي ذلك اليوم من أهل القبور في عسكر الموتى لا يستطيع أن يزيد في حسنة ولا أن يمحو سيئة.

فإذا انتبه العبد في أوان صحته وفراغه وشبابه أمكنه استدراك الفائتات والتخلص من التبعات.

وفي الحديث نعمتان مغبون فيهما كثير من الناس الصحة والفراغ.

وفي الحديث أيضا اغتنم خمسا قبل خمس شبابك قبل هرمك وصحتك قبل سقمك وحياتك قبل مماتك وفراغك قبل شغلك ودنياك قبل آخرتك.

فإنك لا تعلم ما اسمك غدا.

Principle Three: Repentance

If the servant awakens from heedlessness, they can prepare for what awaits them with sincere repentance (*tawbah*) even if they are already repentant. Allāh says, "O you who have believed, repent to Allāh with sincere repentance".

Hence, He orders the believers to repent while they are already repentant, for those who enter upon the path of the elite must renew their sincere repentance, after learning the various rulings of this awakening, which is to perform a complete ablution, go out to a desolate or private place in order to be alone and without distraction, and then pray two units of prayer in which the standing, bowing, and prostration is lengthy. Once finished, they humble themselves before their Lord ﷻ turning in repentance to Him, reverentially fearful of Him, submissive to His authority like one who says, "My Lord, I have come to You fleeing from liabilities, repentant to You, remorseful for my neglect of You, having squandered Your rights and embarked upon what You prohibited, resolved to reform my condition, preparing for my arrival to You, there is no other Lord in which I place my hopes other than You, so pardon me, O Most Merciful".

Along with that, the legislated supplication should be said for indeed it is preferred over all others and more virtuous, which is, "the master supplication of forgiveness, 'O Allāh, You are my Lord. There is no god but You. You have created me, and I am Your servant—and I am upon Your covenant and promise as best I can. I seek refuge in You from the worst of what I have done. I fully admit to You Your blessings upon me, and I fully admit to You all my sins. So, forgive me, for there is none to forgive sins but You.'"

They are to repeat this and whatever else Allāh the Most High grants them until their heart is fearfully submissive, their inner-being is humbled, and they weep; for that, by the will of Allāh the Most High, is the sign of accepted repentance.

الأصل الثالث التوبة

فإذا استيقظ العبد من غفلته استعد لما بين يديه بالتوبة النصوح وإن كان تائبا قال الله تعالى ﴿يا أيها الذين آمنوا توبوا إلى الله توبة نصوحا﴾.

فأمر المؤمنين بالتوبة وهم تائبون والداخل في طريقة الخصوص لا بد له من إحداث توبة صحيحة بعد حصول أحكام هذا اليقظة وهو أن يتوضأ وضوءا كاملا ويخرج إلى براز من الأرض أو مكان خلوة ليخلو سره عن شاغل ثم يصلي ركعتين يطيل قيامهما وركوعهما وسجودهما فإذا سلم منهما إلى ربه عز وجل تائبا إليه خاشعا له خاضعا لقهره مثل أن يقول يا رب جئتك هاربا من الديون تائبا إليك نادما على ما فرطت في جنبك من تضييع حقوقك وارتكاب مناهيك عازما على إصلاح الحال والتأهب للقدوم عليك وليس لي رب أرجوه سواك فتب علي يا أرحم الراحمين.

وليقل الدعاء المشروع مع ذلك فإنه أولى من غيره وأفضل وهو سيد الإستغفار اللّهم أنت ربي لا إله إلا أنت خلقتني وأنا عبدك أنا على عهدك ووعدك ما استطعت أعوذ بك من شر ما صنعت أبوء لك بنعمتك علي وأبوء بذنبي فاغفر لي إنه لا يغفر الذنوب إلا أنت.

فيردد هذا وغيره مما يفتحه الله تعالى حتى يخشع قلبه ويخضع سره ويبكي فذلك علامة قبول التوبة إن شاء الله تعالى.

Preceding this repentance they must be truly resolved to approaching Allāh ﷻ by way of perpetual obedience and evasion of opposition to Him as if they have dedicated themselves to Allāh ﷻ and renounced all that He despises, throwing themselves before Him, crying for help and filled with remorse, resolved to perform everything which He has obligated or encouraged and to abandon every prohibition, form of opposition, and disparaged thing be it major or minor.

Their aspiration should be to have the capacity to fulfill the command of Allāh ﷻ, not leaving a single practice which Allāh ﷻ has ordered, and not committing a single prohibited or disdained act. Rather, they do everything which Allāh has commanded and refrain from everything Allāh ﷻ has prohibited. This is sincere repentance and they are to continue like this until they can find the signs of acceptance in their heart.

From there, with the decree of that aspiration, they seek to be upright for the sake of Allāh ﷻ both inwardly and outwardly, embark upon all other endeavors, inwardly and outwardly, and if they slip up or fall into sin, they are to return to repentance just as before.

وليقدم على هذه التوبة العزم الصحيح على الدخول على الله عز وجل بدوام طاعته ومجانبة مخالفته كأنه قد قدم نفسه لله عز وجل وتنصل من جميع ما يكرهه قد ألقى بنفسه بين يديه مستصرخا نادما عازما على أن يقوم له بكل حق أوجبه أو ندم إليه عازما على ترك جميع المناهي والمخالفات والمكروهات دق أو جل.

وليكن عزمه على أن يستوعب القيام بأمر الله عز وجل لا يترك خصلة واحدة أمره الله عز وجل بها ولا يرتكب خصلة من المناهي والمكروهات بل يقوم بكل شيء أمره الله به ويجتنب كل شيء نهاه الله عز وجل فهذه هي التوبة النصوح فلا يبرح في موضعه ذلك حتى يجد آثار القبول في قلبه.

ثم يقوم من موضعه مستصحبا لحكم ذلك العزم الذي عزم عليه من الاستقامة لله عز وجل ظاهرا وباطنا في سائر المساعي الظاهرة والباطنة ومتى زل أو أخطأ عاد إلى التوبة كما تقدم.

Principle Four: Accountability

If the servant repents, their repentance will not last into the future without accountability.

Accountability begins by making up for everything that has been missed including fasts and prayers and to restore rights, acts of oppression, and liabilities. They are to try and remember every prayer and fast they missed from the time of puberty to the present day and make them up. They are to think about every right that is due and restore them. And they are not to stop until nothing remains so that their conscience is free from all obligatory rights of Allāh ﷻ along with all the rights associated with mankind. At that point, their heart will be released from those shackles and bonds and will then have a place in the gardens of the righteous.

Then they are to take themselves to account regarding the actions of their seven limbs: the eyes, ears, tongue, stomach, sexual organ, hands, and feet, from sunrise to sunset and then from sunset to sunrise.

They are to protect their tongue from every form of speech which does not possess reward or contain some type of needed worldly or spiritual benefit.

They are to protect their eyes from every impermissible sight, especially the young and fair, and women permitted to marry. Doing so is the coitus of the eyes. They should refrain from gazing even when not associated with desire because it serves as a gateway to desire. They are to put an end to gazing upon anything which does not possess reward or contain some type of needed worldly or spiritual benefit.

They are to protect their hearing because the one who listens is the cohort of the one speaking. They are not to listen to anything which does not possess reward or contain some type of needed worldly or spiritual benefit.

الأصل الرابع المحاسبة

والعبد إذا تاب لا تستقيم توبته بالمستقبل إلا بالمحاسبة.

وأول المحاسبة أن يقضي ما عليه من الفوائت من صوم أو صلاة ويؤدي ما قبله من الحقوق والمظالم والديون فيتفكر ويتذكر كل صلاة فائته أو صوم فاته من أيام البلوغ إلى يومه هذا فيقضيه ويتفكر في كل حق كان قبله فؤديه فلا يبرح حتى تبرأ ساحته ويخلص ذمته من كل حق وجب عليه لله عز جل ومن كل حق تعلق بذمته للآذميين فنعد ذلك ينطلق قلبه من القيود والأغلال ويكون له في ميدان الصالحين مجال.

ثم يحاسب نفسه في حركات جوارحه السبع من حين تطلع الشمس إلى أن تغيب ومن غروبها إلى أن تطلع وهي حركات العين الأذن واللسان والبطن والفرج واليد والرجل.

فيحفظ اللسان من كل كلام لا يثاب عليه أو لا يترتب عليه مصلحة دينية ولا دنيوية مما يحتاج إليه.

ويحفظ العين عن كل نظر محرم خصوصا إلى المرد الملاح أو النساء الأجانب فذلك هو زنا النظر ويجتنب النظر ولو بغير شهوة فإن ذلك ذريعة إلى الشهوة ويحسم مادة النظر عن كل شيء لا يثاب عليه ولا يترب عليه مصلحة دينية ولا دنيوية مما يحتاج إليه.

وكذلك يحفظ سمعه فإن المستمع شريك القائل فلا يسمع إلا ما يثاب عليه أو يترتب عليه مصلحة دينية أو دنيوية مما يحتاج إليه.

They are to guard their stomach from the impermissible and doubtful for "every substance reaped from the impermissible is most deserving of Hellfire". Likewise, how is the one who consumes doubtful matters able to enlighten their heart?! How will they purify their deeds?!

They must also safeguard their chastity and protect their hands and feet from every legally illicit and disdained act. When they commit a sin or slip, they are to repent, and their repentance will expunge their crimes leaving their heart polished and radiant.

From the categories of accountability is having goodwill for the faithful. They are to love for them what they love for themselves in all transactions; buying and selling, and thus they do not cheat a Muslim and they give counsel when it is requested.

Likewise, from the categories of accountability is enjoining the good if possible as well as prohibiting evil with gentleness, compassion, and polite instruction. The goal is to display goodwill to the Muslim and to see to their benefit and salvation and not simply to fulfill the trust of disapproval. They are also to refrain from harshness that distresses the hearts, unless, O Allāh, there is a need for it while knowing it will be of benefit. Allāh says, "O Prophet, strive against the disbelievers and the hypocrites, and be tough with them". He also said, "And lower your wing to the believers". Particularly if they see someone exposing their private area (*makshūf al-ʿawrah*) in the bathhouses, they should alert them to it if they are able and if they see someone oppressed, they should strive to assist them if possible.

In general, accountability includes the performance of everything Allāh ﷻ has obligated while refraining from every prohibition He ﷻ has prohibited. If they can be consistent with this directive, they will fulfill the directive of repentance in the future with hopes that Allāh will replace the sins of someone of this nature with good deeds. Allāh says, "Except for those who repent, believe and do righteous work. For them Allāh will replace their evil deeds with good. And ever is Allāh Forgiving and Merciful".

وكذلك يصون بطنه عن الحرام والشبهات فكل جسم نبت من حرام فالنار أولى به وآكل الشبهات كيف يتنور قلبه؟ أم كيف يزكو عمله؟

وكذلك يحفظ الفرج واليدين والرجلين عن جميع محرمات الشرع ومكروهاته ومتى أخطأ أو زل تاب فيمحو بالتوبة ما جناه فينصقل بالتوبة قلبه و يتنور.

ومن أقسام المحاسبة الأمر بالمعروف إذا أمكن والنهي عن المنكر مثله بالرفق وحسن الإرشاد والتلطف يكون غرضه نصح المسلم ونفعه ونجاته لا مجرد تخليصه من عهدة الإنكار ويجتنب فيه من التغليظة الموحشة للقلوب اللّهم إلا إذا أحوج الأمر إلى ذلك وعلم أنه يفيد قال الله تعالى ﴿يا أيها النبي جاهد الكفار والمنافقين واغلظ عليهم﴾.

وقال الله تعالى ﴿واخفض جناحك للمؤمنين﴾.

خصوصا إذا رأى في الحمام مكشوف العورة فلينهه ما استطاع وكذلك إذا رأى مظلوما يجتهد على نصره إذا أمكن.

وفي الجملة فالمحاسبة تستوعب القيام بكل أمر وجب لله عز وجل ومجانبة كل نهي نهى الله عز وجل عنه فإذا استصحب هذا الحكم فقد قام بحكم التوبة في المستقبل ويرجى لمثله أن يبدل الله سيئات حسنات قال الله تعالى ﴿إلا من تاب وآمن وعمل عملا صالحا فألائك يبدل الله سيئاتهم حسنات﴾.

Principle Five: Sincerity

Sincerity (*al-ikhlāṣ*) is to inspect all their outward endeavors and dedicate them to Allāh ﷻ. Likewise, they are to inspect their inward actions such as their aspirations, resolutions, and intentions and sincerely dedicate them to Allāh ﷻ.

They must learn about the intention (*niyyah*) and how it is set aright. If they understand it, they will not do anything without it; not speaking, eating, or walking without an intention.

The intention, as an idiom of the mystics, is the intent of something based on the perceived fear of punishment or desired reward, or to venerate the command of Allāh ﷻ. It is as if they perceive two things together at once. They take note of the deed and what it warrants with Allāh ﷻ in the Hereafter. When these two things are clear in the heart, it formulates a valid intention and its heartfelt experience is precious. None can achieve it except those of purity and insightfulness for it is possible that a servant takes note of the deed and its associated outcome in the Hereafter but does it with the intention of worldly gain. This distinction eludes the people of desire who are incapable of knowing how to purify what is for Allāh ﷻ from what is for themselves and their own world due to the darkness of their hearts and overwhelming impulses.

The servant must inspect the location of intention and sincerity of the heart in their deeds in all hidden and apparent endeavors. They should protect their intention from hypocrisy (*riyāʾ*), considering none of creation regarding their deeds, and protect their hearts from vanity (*ʿujub*) with sincerity, for it is possible that the servant unknowingly become conceited because of their sincerity. It has been reported in a ḥadīth that "Actions are by nothing other than their intentions and everyone shall have what they intend. Therefore, whoever's migration was for Allāh and His messenger, their migration will be for Allāh and His messenger. And, whoever's migration was to achieve something of the world or to marry a woman, their migration will be for what they migrated to".

الأصل الخامس الإخلاص

وهو أن يتفقد مساعيه الظاهرة من الأعمال فيجعلها لله عز وجل خالصا وكذلك يتفقد مساعيه الباطنة من الهمم والعزائم القصود فيجعلها لله عز وجل خالصا.

وليتعلم علم النية وتصحيحها فإذا علمها لا يتحرك إلا بنية ولا يتكلم إلا بنية ولا يأكل إلا بنية ولا يمشي إلا بنية.

والنية على اصطلاح القوم هو قصد الشيء على ملاحظة خوف العقاب أو رجاء الثواب أو التعظيم لأمر الله عز وجل فكأنه يلحظ الشيئين جميعا في آن واحد فيلحظ العمل وما يؤدي إليه عند الله عز وجل في الآخرة فمتى خلصت هاتان الملاحظتان في القلب فهذه هي النية الصحيحة والشعور بها في القلب غزيز لا يخلصه إلا أهل الصفاء بالبصائر الباطنة فقد يلحظ العبد العمل وما يترتب عليه في الآخرة فيقصده لذلك ولشيء آخر من عرض الدنيا ويخفى تميز ذلك على أهل الهوى ويعجزون عن معرفة تخليص ما لله عز وجل عما لأنفسهم ولدنياهم لظلمة قلوبهم وغلبة أهوائهم.

فليتفقد العبد محل النية والإخلاص من قلبه في أعماله وسعاياته الظاهرة والباطنة ويحفظ نيته من الرياء فلا يلحظ بأعماله أحدا من الخلق ويحفظ قلبه من العجب مع الإخلاص فقد يعجب العبد بإخلاصه ولا يشعر وفي الحديث إنما الأعمال بالنيات وإنما لامرئ ما نوى فمن كانت هجرته إلى الله ورسوله فهجرته إلى الله ورسوله ومن كانت هجرته إلى دنيا يصيبها أو امرأة يتزوجها فهجرته إلى ما هاجر إليه.

They should therefore be busy with knowledge through repetition, revision, and research for the sake of Allāh ﷻ. Their sincere engrossment in knowledge will then be the greatest of virtuous action with Allāh. It is the endeavor of the learned, those whose praises are made by the fish in the sea as has been narrated in a ḥadīth which states, "The learned are the inheritors of the prophets. They inherit neither dīnār nor dirham, they inherit knowledge, and so whoever takes hold of it has taken an ample portion".

The difference between honesty (*ṣidq*) and sincerity is that honesty is to resolve yourself wholeheartedly to a single thing to the point that you are solely devoted to it so that you do it completely and faithfully for Allāh.

Sincerity is to remove your sights and attention from all others, including worldly gain, position, leadership, or recognition, besides Allāh ﷻ in that action.

Whoever is able to combine between both honesty and sincerity in their actions and endeavors, both outward and inward, their deeds will be sound, and will ascend, by divine will, to Allāh who has said, "good words rise up to Him and He lifts up the righteous deed".

The sign of the honest, when they devote a duty to Allāh ﷻ such as prayer, fasting, hajj, enjoining the good, forbidding the evil, or any other charge; or when they devote a prohibition such as lowering the gaze, refraining from doubtful food, or turning away from listening to the foul and lude; or initially devotes themselves to Allāh ﷻ to embark upon a voluntary or recommended deed, they do so striving to their full capacity just like the obedient and faithful servant does for their master when they are sent on an errand, striving to retrieve for their master the best and most elegant of what is demanded as is the case with prohibitions, they strive, at full capacity, to avoid even its nuances and subtleties.

فيجعل اشتغاله بالعلم من التكرار والمذاكرة والبحث لله عز وجل فيكون باشتغاله بالعلم على الإخلاص من أكبر الأعمال الفاضلة عند الله وهو عمل العلماء الذين تسبح لهم الحيتان في البحار كما جاء في الحديث والعلماء ورثة الأنبياء لم يورثوا دينارا ولا درهما إنما ورثوا العلم فمن أخذه أخذ بحظ وافر.

والفرق بين الصدق والإخلاص أن الصدق هو اجتماعك على قصد الشيء وعمله بجميعك بحيث لا يتخلف عنه منك شيء فلا تعمله ببعضك بل بكلك ناصحا لله فيه.

والإخلاص هو تخليص نظرك في ذلك العمل عن رؤية سوى الله عز وجل وملاحظة غيره من دنيا أو جاه أو رئاسة أو طلب منزلة.

فمن اجتمع في أعماله ومساعيه الظاهرة والباطنة الصدق والإخلاص استقام عمله ورفع مع المشيئة إلى الله قال تعالى ﴿إليه يصعد الكلم الطيب والعمل الصالح يرفعه﴾.

فعلامة الصادق إذا توجه الله عز وجل عليه أمر مثل صلاة أو صام أو حج أو أمر بمعروف أو نهي عن منكر أو غير ذلك من الأوامر أو توجه عليه نهي مثل غض نظر أو اجتناب طعام شبهة أو تعرية سمع عن الفواحش والخنا أو توجه هو إلى الله عز وجل ابتداء بعمل من الأعمال المندوبة أو المستحبة أن يبذل في ذلك العمل جهده وطاقته كما ينصح العبد البار الناصح لسيده إذا بعثه في مهم فإنه يجتهد على أن يأخذ لسيده أحسن الحوائج وأظرفها وكذلك يكون عند المناهي يبذل جهده وطاقته في التوقي عن دقائقها ورقائقها.

This is the way of those faithful (*nāṣiḥ*) to Allāh ﷻ in their actions, they spare no expense in their efforts and perform them incorporating body, spirit, mind, heart, and soul.

The faithful are therefore honest and if sincerity is added, so that they do not incorporate in their aim (*qaṣd*) anyone besides Allāh ﷻ, their honesty will be perfected to the level of their sincerity which will also serve as evidence to the honest nature of their aim.

Whoever is honest in their action but not honest in their aim is not honest.

Therefore, every completely honest person is sincere but not vice versa. It is possible for someone sincere, who has not intended anyone besides Allāh in their action, to not exert themselves entirely in the performance of the deed.

Faithfulness to Allāh ﷻ in deeds is the grand elixir, with it, Allāh ﷻ, if He so wills, opens the locks of prophetic states and lofty stations for the servant. So, whoever interacts with Allāh faithfully, Allāh will be faithful to them which will be a sufficient reward in this life and the Hereafter. The supporting evidence for this is the ḥadīth, "Whoever draws near to Me by a hand span, I will draw near to him by the span of a forearm".

Likewise, the faithful will be faithfully rewarded "an appropriate recompense".

Some have said that below these three there lies a treasure of which none knows its magnitude save those who are deserving. It is the letters Nūn, Ṣād, and Ḥa, so engrave them in your heart and adhere to their directives so long as you are alive in order that you may reap its fruits, God willing, now and in the future.

فهذا الناصح لله عز وجل في أعماله لم يتخلف منه ذلك العمل جهد بل عمل ذلك العمل لله بجسمه ونفسه وعقله وقلبه وروحه.

وهذا الناصح هو الصادق فإن انضاف إليه الإخلاص بحيث لم يشرك في قصده به أحدا غير الله عز وجل كمل صدقه أيضا فيه كمال إخلاصه فكان ذلك دليلا منه على صدقه في القصد أيضا.

ومن صدق في عمله ولم يصدق في قصده لم يكن صادقا كامل الصدق مخلص ولا ينعكس فقد يكون الملخص الذي لم يلحظ غير الله في عمله لم يبذل له كله في ذلك العمل.

وهذا النصح لله عز وجل في الأعمال هو الإكسير الأعظم به يفتح الله عز وجل إذا شاء على العبد مغالق الأحوال السنية والمقامات العلية فمن عامل الله بالنصح نصحه الله وكفى بذلك ثوابا في الدنيا والآخرة والدليل عليه الحديث من تقرب مني شبرا تقربت منه ذراعا. كذلك الناصح يجازي بالنصح ﴿جزاء وفاقا﴾.

وبغض الناس يقول تحت هذه الثلاثة كنز لا يعرف قدره إلا أهله وهو ن ص ح فانقشها في قلبك والتزم حكمها ما عشت تجد ثمرتها إن شاء الله عاجلا وآجلا.

Principle Six: Inner Manners of Prayer

Prayer is the gauge of states and hearts. While in it, the servant's state and station of faith becomes obvious be it of love, fear, hope, reverence, proximity, presence, or connection to Allāh. The signs of these will become clear in the prayer.

Whoever's prayer is filled with disturbance, to the point that they do not understand what they are reading, do not find delight in the presence of and interaction with Allāh ﷻ, there is no state nor station, their prayer is like that of the laity, and they are simply going through the motions while their heart is wandering in worldly thoughts and reflections, then they have not approached Allāh with their heart nor have they obtained the required reverence for success just as Allāh the Most High said, "Successful are the believers. Those who are filled with reverence in prayer. Those who shun idle speech". They have not mentally turned away from idle speech even though their tongue is reciting, and their body is bowing and prostrating.

As for the elite, the chosen people of Allāh ﷻ, when they head to the place of prayer, they intend to visit Allāh ﷻ in His house, answering His caller, which is the mu'adhin, seeing themselves as Allāh's guest, intending to fulfill one of Allāh's obligations, and to be present before Him. When they say 'Allāhu akbar', there is nothing in their heart greater than Allāh that can distract them. They then stand in front of Allāh ﷻ with a present heart, knowing that Allāh ﷻ sees them and their position, that He hears their hidden discourse, and knows the intent and aim of their conscience. They say "All praise belongs to Allāh, Lord of the worlds", in a discourse with their Munificent Lord, and when they reach "It is You alone we worship" their heart becomes ever more present for that is the address of the present to the attendees.

الأصل السادس آداب الصلاة الباطنة

والصلاة محك الأحوال والقلوب فيها يظهر حال العبد ومقامه من إيمانه إن كان محبا أو خائفا أو راجيا أو ذا خشية أو ذا قرب أو ذا حضور أو ذا تعلق بالله ظهرت آثار ذلك في الصلاة.

ومن احتوشته الوسواس في الصلاة بحيث لا يفقه ما يقرأ فيها ولا يجد لذة الحضور والمعاملة مع الله عز وجل فيها ولا حال له ولا مقام وصلاته صلاة العوام يصلي بجسمه وقلبه يجول في أفكار الدنيا وتدبير أمورها فلم يقبل على الله بقلبه ولا حصل له الخشوع الموجب للفلاح كما قال الله تعالى ﴿قد أفلح المؤمنون. الذين هم في صلاتهم خاشعون. والذين هم عن اللغو معرضون﴾. فلم يعرض عن اللغو بفكره وإن كان لسانه تاليا وجسمه راكعا وساجدا.

أما الخواص أهل الله عز وجل إذا توجه أحدهم إلى المسجد فينوي زيارة الله عز وجل في بيته وإجابة داعيه وهو المؤذن يرى أنه داعي الله وينوي إقامة فريضة الله والحضور بين يدي الله فإذا قال الله أكبر فلا يجد في قلبه أكبر من الله فيتوسوس به ثم يقف بين يدي الله عز وجل حاضر القلب عالما بأن الله عز وجل يراه ويرى مكانه ويسمع نجواه ويعلم قصده ونيته في ضميره فيقول ﴿الحمد لله رب العالمين﴾ مناجيا بذلك لربه الكريم فإذا بلغ ﴿إياك نعبد﴾ حضر حضورا آخر أخص من الحضور الأول فإن ذلك خطاب الحاضر للحاضرين

They then recite the Qur'ān, pondering and open-minded, understanding what Allāh ﷻ intended as if they were reciting to Allāh ﷻ or as if they were listening to Allāh ﷻ, paying close attention to His promise and warning and His incitement of fear and His admonition. Every word of Allāh ﷻ has a meaning which requires of His servants a particular type of servitude be it fear, hope, remembrance, credence, learning a lesson, love, longing, craving, dread, proximity, or connection; they therefore understand the intent of Allāh ﷻ and establish the servitude essential to its associated meaning. In doing so, as Allāh ﷻ says, they "recite it with its true recital. They are the ones who believe in it".

Among them are those, from the verses, who seek the meanings of the Speaker's attributes. Because of that, in their hearts, they are blessed with the witnessing (*al-muhsāhdah*); for indeed He, the Glorified, speaks with powerful, merciful, mighty, and compelling words resulting in the gnostic's heart a manifestation of every attribute's meaning which describes the Speaker in each verse. Thus, prayer, recitation, and understanding of Allāh ﷻ are brought together for the gnostic along with an internal study of the grandeur of Allāh's ﷻ attributes.

When it comes to prayer, people are of four categories:

There are those who are heedless in their prayer. They are the people of distractions and worldly engagement. Their thoughts lure them to the world and so they have obtained nothing of the prayer except for whatever they have managed to capture.

The second group, their hearts are absent and so they call them back to attention when it roams. Every time they wander into the valleys of the world, while standing before Allāh, they bring them back. This is the prayer of the seeker (*murīd*) who is exerting effort and fighting with their enemy and human spirit (*nafs*). Sometimes they are victorious and others they are defeated, luring their spirit to the truth at times and their spirit luring them away from Allāh at others.

ثم يقرأ القرآن بتدبر وتفهم يفهم عن الله عز وجل مراده كأنه يقرأ على الله عز وجل أو يسمعه من الله عز وجل فينتبه لوعد الله ووعيده وتخويفه وتحذيره فإن الله عز وجل في كل كلمة معنى يقتضي بها من عباده عبودية خاصة من خوف أو رجاء أو ذكر أو تصديق أو اتعاظ أو محبة أو شوق أو رغبة أو رهبة أو قرب أو اتصال فيفهم عن الله عز وجل مراده ويقوم بما يقتضيه المعنى من العبودية فيكون في ذلك كما قال الله عز وجل ﴿يتلونه حق تلاوته أولائك يؤمنون به﴾.

وفيهم من يستجلي من الآيات معاني صفات المتكلم فيرزق بذلك المشاهدة بقلبه فإنه سبحانه يتكلم بكلام عظيم ورحيم وجبار وملك قهار فيظهر لقلب العارف في كل آية الوصف الذي ظهر المتكلم به في ذلك المعنى فيجمع لهذا العبد العارف بين الصلاة والتلاوة والفهم عن الله عز وجل والوقوف بسره على عظمة صفات الله عز وجل.

واعلم أن الناس في الصلاة أربع فرق منهم من يصلي صلاة الغافلين وهم أهل الوسواس وجواذب الأفكار الدنيوية تجذبهم الأفكار إلى الدنيا فهؤلاء ليس لهم من صلاتهم إلا ما عقلوا منها.

والفرقة الثانية قلوبهم غائبة فيطالبونهم بالحضور وهي تشرد كلما شردت إلى أودية الدنيا من بين يدي الله عز وجل ردوها وهذا صلاة المريدين المجاهدين المحاربين لعدوهم ونفوسهم وأحدهم غالب تارة ومغلوب أخرى يجذبون نفوسهم إلى الحق تارة وتجذبهم النفوس إلى غير الله أخرى.

The third group, their hearts are tempered and free from their spirit's captivity. They are praying, reciting, comprehending, and discoursing. It articulates the takbīr and al-fatiḥah while the tongue is interpreting what has settled in the heart of Allāh's ﷻ worship, unlike those previously mentioned. They read with their tongues and with them lure their hearts to agreement and attendance. This group, their hearts are speaking while their tongues act as their interpreters.

The fourth group, when they enter prayer, they disappear into the epiphanies of their hearts which result from the divine attributes' impacts such as awe, reverence, and exaltation. Their hearts and souls have been seized, carried away by the light of sublimity while the intimate discourse and understanding remains in the locus of the purified immaculate spirit. This is because their spirits have taken residence in their hearts and their hearts in their souls and so this is the prayer of those who draw near.

May Allāh make us of them. Amīn.

O seeker, look within yourself. To which group do you belong? Treat your heart and you will progressively elevate from the lower levels to the highest. Be in a state of need of Allāh the Most High and in doing so you will arrive by His will.

The servant when bowing is the same. They are lowered before The Truth ﷻ, they are submissive and humbled both inwardly and outwardly in order that their hearts be characterized as proverbially bowing, which is the image of humility and submission, just as they are characterized by the outward image while bowing. At that point, the outside is aligned with the inside and so their innermost being is equal to their outer-being. This is different from those who bow with their body physically, but their heart does not submit spiritually as if part of them has bowed without the other. They bowed with their body, a part of the seen world, but their heart, a part of the hidden world, has not.

الفرقة الثالثة قد لطفت قلوبهم وتخلصت من أسر نفوسهم فهي المصلية والتالية والفاهمة والمناجية هو الناطقة بالتكبير والفاتحة واللسان مترجم عما استكن في القلب من العبادة لله عز وجل بخلاف الذين قبلهم فإنهم يقرأون بألسنتهم ويطالبون قلوبهم بالمواطأة والحضور مع ألسنتهم وهؤلاء قلوبهم هي الناطقة واللسان معبر عنها.

الفرقة الرابعة إذا دخلوا في الصلاة غابوا بما تجلى على قلوبهم من آثار الصفات من الهيبة والإجلال والتعظيم فيخطف قلوبهم وأرواحهم تخطفها أنوار العظمة وتبقى المناجاة والفهم في محل النفس الطاهرة المزكاة لأن نفوسهم صارت في محل القلب والقلب صار في محل الروح والروح في محل القلب وهذه صلاة المقربين جعلنا الله منهم آمين.

فانظر نفسك أيها المريد من أي الفرق الأربع أنت. وعالج قلبك وترق من المراتب النازلة إلى المراتب العالية بالتدرج وافتقر إلى الله تعالى في ذلك تبلغ إن شاء الله تعالى.

وكذلك العبد في الركوع ينحني ويتدلي بين يدي الحق عز وجل خاضعا متواضعا بقلبه وقالبه ليتصف القلب بالانحناء المعنوي الذي هو صورة الذلة الخضوع كما اتصف الظاهر بالانحناء الصوري فيطابق حينئذ ظاهره وباطنه ويستوي سره وعلانيته بخلاف من انحنى بجسمه صورة ولم يخضع بقلبه معنى فكأنه ركع بنصفه وتخلف عن الركوع النصف الآخر ركع بجسمه الذي هو من عالم الشهادة ولم يركع بقلبه الذي هو من عالم الغيب.

Prostration is the same way. And in the tashahhud, they are before Allāh ﷻ in a discourse with Him, asking of Him. When they bow, they do not talk to themselves about rising due to their heart's pleasure and delight found within it. The same goes for prostration. This is from the perfection of the prayer's manners, inner-dimensions, and realities.

A sign of one who has prayed with their heart and soul is their remaining after its conclusion for some time so that their heart and mind can return after being completely submerged and present in the prayer.

Whoever is granted success by Allāh ﷻ in their five prayers in such a way, it is hoped that they will remain in the luminance of prayer until the next and that their days and nights will be inundated and immersed in the radiance of light, both their inner and outer-being inundated in the presence of the Omnipotent King.

وليكن في السجود كذلك وفي التشهد حاضرا بين يدي الله عز وجل مناجيا له سائلا منه وإذا ركع لا يحدث نفسه بالاعتدال لطيبة قلبه فيه ولذته به وكذلك السجود فبذلك من إكمال هيئات الصلاة وأسرارها وحقائقها.

وعلامة من صلى بقلبه وقالبه أن يبقى بعد السلام زمنا ليعود روعه إليه لكمال استغراقه وحضوره في الصلاة.

فمن وفقه الله تعالى للصلوات الخمس على هذه الصفة يرجى له أن يبقى في نور كل صلاة إلى الصلاة الأخرى فلا يزال نهاره وليله مغمورا مغموسا في لوامع الأنوار مغمور الظاهر والناطن في حضرة الملك الجبار.

Principle Seven: Refining Character and Taming and Opposing the Spirit in Order to Practice Noble Manners

This is a pillar of the religion. Noble manners are evident of purification of the spirit (*nafs*) and are from the qualities of the successful. Allāh ﷻ said, "Successful are those who purify it". What this means is to replace innate blameworthy qualities with their opposites—praiseworthy qualities—after becoming cognizant of them.

The first of them is to cleanse the heart of pride (*kibr*) as noted in the ḥadīth, "None with an ounce of pride in the heart shall enter Paradise".

They are to yield to Allāh ﷻ and be humble with the believers just as He, the Most High, says, "They are people who are humble towards the believers and powerful against the disbelievers".

They do not see themselves superior to any of Allāh's ﷻ creatures by way of knowledge or state, but see themselves as lesser than them because their states are hidden with Allāh ﷻ who said, "So do not claim yourselves to be pure; He is most knowing of who fears Him" and "O you who have believed, let not a people ridicule [another] people; perhaps they may be better than them".

They then are to cleanse their heart of jealousy (*hasad*)—envying no one due to what Allāh has bestowed upon them from His bounty—which is to desire the cessation of their blessing and is a quality of the Jews. Allāh said, "Or do they envy people for what Allāh has given them of His bounty?"

الأصل السابع تهذيب الأخلاق ورياضة النفس ومخالفتها للتمرن على مكارم الأخلاق

وهو ركن من أركان الدين وحسن الأخلاق يدل على تزكية النفس وهو من صفات المفلحين قال الله عز وجل ﴿قد أفلح من زكاها﴾.

وذلك عبارة عن تبديل الصفات المذمومة من الجبلة بأضدادها من الصفات المحمودة بعد التفطن لها.

فأول ذلك تنقية القلب عن الكبر ففي الحديث لا يدخل الجنة من في قلبه مثقال ذرة من كبر.

فيتواضع لله عز وجل ويذل للمؤمنين كما قال تعالى ﴿أذلة على المؤمنين أعزة على الكافرين﴾.

فلا يرى نفسه على أحد من خلق الله عز وجل بعلم ولا حال ويرى نفسه دونهم لأن أحوالهم مغيبة عنه عند الله عز وجل قال الله تعالى ﴿فلا تزكوا أنفسكم هو أعلم بمن اتقى﴾ وقال تعالى ﴿يا أيها الذين آمنوا لا يسخر قوم من قوم عسى أن يكونوا خيرا منهم﴾.

ثم تنقية القلب عن الحسد أحدا على ما آتاه الله من فضله بحيث يحب زوال النعمة عنه فذلك من أخلاق اليهود قال الله تعالى ﴿أم يحسدون الناس على ما آتاهم الله من فضله﴾.

Rather, they are to love for everyone what they love for themselves and dislike for them what they dislike for themselves. When they feel envy in their heart, they extinguish it, purify their heart of it, despise it, and pray that the one they are envious of will receive the blessing in full. This is what will strengthen them.

Replacing the quality within themselves is up to Allāh ﷻ which occurs by way of purification of the heart by actualizing piety (*taqwa*) and asceticism (*zuhd*). Whoever observes piety and asceticism, their heart will be purified of foul manners by the will of Allāh ﷻ.

There are some scholars who have included this with the major sins, declaring it juxtaposed to the major outward sins, in that its punishment in the Hereafter will be like their punishment.

Formulating evil assumptions is also included in those vile traits and therefore should be mostly avoided as Allāh ﷻ has ordered.

Foul manners are of two categories: there are those which are juxtaposed to outward prohibitions and others which are juxtaposed to the abhorred.

The first category includes things like pride, conceit, fear of poverty, displeasure with what has been decreed, spitefulness, malice, deception, seeking status, disdain for the poor, love of leadership, enmity, hating for other than Allāh's sake, chauvinism of the self, disdain for the needy, insolence and ingratitude, venerating the wealthy within the heart due to their riches, despising the poor in the heart due to their poverty, pride and arrogance in one's appearance, attributes, and knowledge etc.; endearing one's self to people with what Allāh does not like, competing with others in worldly pursuits and positions, boasting and fame, arrogantly turning away from the truth, knowingly defending falsehood to advocate for one's own self, remaining quiet about the truth out of fear of losing one's position, being weary or feigning capability of Allāh's directive,

بل يحب لكل أحد ما يحب لنفسه ويكره له ما يكره لنفسه ومتى أحس من قلبه بحسد نفاه ونقى قلبه منه وكرهه ودعا للمحسود بتمام النعمة فذلك الذي يمكنه أما تبديل ذلك من نفسه فهو إلى الله عز وجل وإنما يكون ذلك عند طهارة القلب بتحقيق التقوى والزهد فمن حقق التقوى والزهد صفا قلبه من خبائث الأخلاق بمشيئة الله عز وجل.

وبعض العلماء يعد هذه كبائر الذنوب ويجعلها بإزاء الكبائر الظاهرة بمعنى أن عقوبتها في الآخرة كعقوبتها.

ومن ذلك الخبث وسوء الظن فليجتنب كثيرا منه كما أمر الله عز وجل.

وخبائث الأخلاق قسمان قسم منها قام بإزاء المحارم الظاهرة والقسم الثاني بإزاء المكروهات.

فالقسم الأول كالكبر والعجب وخوف الفقر وسخط المقدور والغل والحقد والغش وطلب العلو وطلب المنزلة والأنفة من الفقر وحب الرئاسة والعداوة والبغضة لغير الله والحمية للنفس والأنفة من الفقر والأشر والبطر والتعظيم للأغنياء بالقلب من أجل غناهم والاستهانة بالفقراء بالقلب من أجل فقرهم والفخر والخيلاء في الهيئة والصفات والعلم وغير ذلك والتحبب إلى الناس بما لا يحب الله والتنافس في الدنيا والمناصب والرياء والسمعة والإعراض عن الحق استكبارا والانتصار للباطل مع العلم به لنصرة النفس والسكوت عن الحق خشية سقوط المنزلة والتملل والاقتدار في أمر الله

adornment with the religion for the sake of creation to gain their veneration, flattery, being praised under false pretenses, forgetting Allāh's favor, blindness to His benevolence, being brotherly publicly with enmity in the heart, feeling secure from the removal of what has been given, reliance upon obedience, plotting and betrayal, deception, bad manners, belittling the believer, making light of their honor, and a lack of shame and mercy.

The second category, which is juxtaposed to the abhorred disliked acts, includes love of this world, love of life in order to take pleasure in this world, the desire to delve into that which is of no concern, excessive talking, excessive food, boasting, the absence of sadness in the heart, covetousness and high expectations, loss of self-worth when their words are rejected, surliness and hard-heartedness, heedlessness and a sense of security, being happy with this world and sad due to its loss, delight with creation and lonely when unable to see them, argumentation, rudeness, recklessness, rashness, and rage.

If a person becomes aware of any of that within themselves, they should despise it, be wary of it, and impose upon themselves their opposites as an act dedicated to Allāh in order that it becomes second nature.

They are to replace pride with humility, conceit with acknowledgement of favor, fear of poverty with reliance upon Allāh ﷻ, disdain for what has been decreed with pleasure with Allāh ﷻ, malice with a pure heart, the same goes for malice and deception, seeking status with seeking the Hereafter and what lies with Allāh, disdain for the poor with abhorrence of one's spirit due to the robes of the destitute it actually wears, enmity with affection, and hatred with love. In this manner, what is found within the spirit should be replaced with its opposite until Allāh extends help and the heart is reformed in every way in the station of divine supervision (*maqām al-murāqabah*) after such favor.

والتزين للمخلوقين بالدين ليعظموه والمداهنة وأن يمدح بما لم يفعل ونسيان نعمة الله تعالى والعمى عن إحسانه واتخاذ إخوان العلانية على عداوة السر والأمن لسلب ما أعطي والاتكال على الطاعة والمكر والخيانة والخادعة وسوء الخلق واستحقار المؤمن والاستخفاف بحرمته وقلة الحياء والرحمة.

القسم الثاني ما قام بإزاء المكروهات الظاهرة وذلك كحب الدنيا وحب الحياة للتنعم في الدنيا وشهوة الخوض فيما لا يعني وكثرة الكلام وفضول الطعام والصلف وافتقاد الحزن من القلب والحرص وطول الأمل وذهاب مال النفس إذا رد عليه قوله والفظاظة وغلظ القلب والغفلة والأمن والفرح بالدنيا والحزن على فوتها والأنس بالمخلوقين والوحشة إذا عجز عن رؤيتهم والمراء في الكلام والجفاء والطيش والعجلة والحدة.

فإذا انتبه الإنسان من نفسه لشيء من ذلك فليكرهه ويتقيه ويتخلق بضده تكلفا يعامل الله بذلك ليصير عادة وطبعا.

فيبدل من نفسه الكبر بالتواضع والعجب برؤية المنة وخوف الفقر بالوثوق بالله عز وجل وسخط المقدور بالرضا عن الله عز وجل والغل بسلامة القلب والحقد والغش مثله وطلب العلو بطلب الآخرة وما عند الله والأنفة من الفقر بإكراه النفس على ما يظهر منه من زي الفقراء والعداوة بالألفة والبغضة بالمودة وأمثال ذلك يبدل من نفسه كل وصف بضده حتى يأتي الله بالمدد منه فينصلح القلب بجميع أرجائه في مقام المراقبة بعد هذا الفضل

Then, and only then, noble character is likely to flow from the heart in a natural way and not merely something acquired. The cause of that lies in the heart's connection to divine radiance after it has been purified of its qualities. Success is with Allāh.

فحينئذ يرجى أن تفيض من قلبه مكارم الأخلاق طبعا لا تطبعا وسبب ذلك اتصال الأنوار الإلـهية بقلبه بعد طهارته وصفائه وبالله التوفيق.

Principle Eight: Divine Supervision, Description of it States, and Benefits

When the servant repents and settles all rights, is truly accountable and safeguards their limbs, habitually does what is found in this booklet—to the point that it becomes second nature, embedded within, discomforted when something slips by or due to inconsistency—they will be outwardly sound, aligned with Allāh's directive, and fulfilling His rights without suffering. Initially, however, struggle and hardship is essential.

If they can rise to such an occasion and possess a connection with their Lord ﷻ which they are aware of, they will know, based on that, their growth, decline, and stagnation. Without a doubt, they cannot escape from these three states; they are either growing, declining, or stagnating.

At this juncture, their piety, accountability, and care moves into their heart. They then remain fearing Allāh with their hearts as they do with their limbs, caring for their heart just as they hold their tongue and gaze accountable out of fear for Allāh ﷻ and shy from His taking note of what their heart contains and looking at them and their deeds to find what is displeasing. Allāh ﷻ says, "Allāh knows what is within yourselves, so beware of Him", "And leave what is apparent of sin and what is concealed thereof", and "And conceal your speech or publicize it; indeed, He is Knowing of that within the breasts. Does He who created not know".

This is the first step along the path of the elite. What came before this, because it focused on what is outward and physical, which is for all the believers, was the way of the masses. So, if they work on rectifying and treating their heart, they will enter the path of those with certainty.

الأصل الثامن المراقبة وصفة أحوالها وثمراتها

العبد إذا تاب إلى الله وتخلص من الحقوق وأدى حق المحاسبة ورعاية الجوارح وقام بما في هذه الكراسة واعتاده يحيث يصير جميع ذلك طبيعا راسخا فيه يتأذى إذا فاته شيء من ذلك أو لم ينتظم له أمره فيه فيستقيم حينئذ ظاهره على أمر الله والقيام بحقه فلا يحتاج في إقامته إلى مكابدة ففي أول الأمر لا يد من المجاهدة والمكابدة.

فإذا استقام على ذلك وصار له مع ربه عز وجل رابطة يعرفها ويعرف بها زيادته ونقصانه ومن وقوفه فإنه لا يخلو من أحد هذه الأحوال الثلاثة إما أن يكون في زيادة أو نقصان أو وقوف.

فعند ذلك تنتقل تقواه ومحاسبته ورعايته إلى قلبه فيبقى يتقي الله في قلبه كما يتقيه في جوارحه يراعي قلبه كما يراعي المحاسب لسانه ونظره خوفا من الله عز وجل وحياء من اطلاعه على قلبه ونظره إليه وعلمه به فيجد فيه ما يكرهه وقد قال الله عز وجل ﴿الله يعلم ما في أنفسكم فاحذروه﴾ وقال تعالى ﴿وذروا ظاهر الإثم وباطنه﴾ وقال تعالى ﴿وأسروا قولكم أو اجهروا به إنه عليم بذات الصدور. ألا يعلم من خلق﴾.

فهذا أول طريق الخصوص وما قبله من طريق العموم لأنه في الظواهر والأبدان وهو لعموم المؤمنين فإذا اشتغل بإصلاح القلب ومعالجته دخل في طريق الموقنين

This is because it requires intense certainty that Allāh ﷻ is aware of them and observing their heart which yields certainty of Him and shyness from Him moments after they realize that shyness of Him in action. They therefore protect their heart from impermissible notions just as they have prevented their limbs from sinful action. They then protect it from meddling and internal dialogue just as they have outwardly protected themselves from wasteful deeds. This is the last level of divine supervision after accountability.

Once they master that and it takes up residence within them, becoming a regular habit and deeply rooted condition—to the point that they no longer need to exert great effort—His supervision will settle in their heart just as accountability has outwardly. Upon this occasion, it is likely that the heart will become a heaven enlightened by the stars of remembrance and pure musings. After perfection of true piety, they will be wary of the impermissible, disdained, and excessive both inwardly and outwardly. Their actions and notions will then become acts of duty, devotion, knowledge, understanding, and remembrance resulting in a change of human nature, their disposition and manners will be overturned and replaced with attributes of the spiritual. Consequently, the servant, by God's decree and conferment, will observe their heart penetrate the realm of the heavens and encounter the obvious truth and knowledge, essence, and absolute nature of certainty.

لأن الموجب لذلك قوة يقينه باطلاع الله عز وجل على قلبه وعلمه به فأكسبه اليقين والحياء منه في اللحظات بعد تحقيق الحياء منه في الحركات فيحفظ قلبه عن خواطر الحرام كما حفظ جوارحه عن حركات الآثام ثم يحفظ قلبه عن الفضول وحديث النفس كما حمى ظاهره عن حركات الفضول وهذا آخر مراتب المراقبة بعد المحاسبة.

فإذا أحكم ذلك وتوطن فيه وصار ذلك له عادة ثابتة وهيئة راسخة بحيث لا يحتاج إلى تكلف وتعمل فحينئذ تستقر مراقبته في القلب كما استقرت محاسبته في الظاهر فعند ذلك يرجى أن يصير القلب سماء يتوقد بنجوم الذكر وصفاء الفكر بعد إكمال حق التقوى فإنه اتقى المحارم والمكاره والفضول من ظاهره وباطنه فصارت حركاته وخطراته حقوقا وعبوديات وعلوما وفهوما وأذكارا فتبدلت منه طباع البشرية وانقلبت سجاياهم وأخلاقها فتبدلت بصفات الروحانيين فعند ذلك يشارف العبد ولوج قلبه لملكوت السماء والمكالمة بصريح الحق وعلم اليقين وعين اليقين وحق اليقين وبمشيئة الله تعالى وتوفيقه.

Principle Nine: The Witnessing, Its Types and Categories

You must understand that whoever takes on the task of learning sacred knowledge has perfected their intellectual constitution. Whoever performs outward deeds based on knowledge has perfected their instinctual human nature. Whoever established the authentic supervision of Allāh ﷻ in their heart has perfected their heart's disposition. The only thing left to complete is their spiritual constitution which is victory that Allāh the Most High grants to His servants who love Him, long for Him, seek His proximity, and have concern for it, day and night, like the jurist does for understanding the law or greater.

If the servant is able to traverse this mentioned path, being truly accountable and true to divine supervision, their outer-piety reaches their inner-self, they are outwardly sound by way of accountability and inwardly so by way of divine supervision, their heart is purified, calm, and made tranquil by way of pure piety and asceticism, it is likely that The Truth ﷻ will rectify the servant by way of allure and shine upon his heart the stars of knowledge, the moons of His monotheism, and the suns of His gnosis.

What The Truth calls His servants and intimate friends to cannot be sequenced, however, the order of divine spectables based on its academic categorization is as follows: gnosis of Allāh ﷻ by way of His actions, gnosis of Him by way of His attributes, and gnosis of His by way of Himself ﷻ.

The first is the opening of the heart to reflection on Allāh's ﷻ blessing, favors, acts, creation, creatures, and command. So, they reflect, think deeply "into the realm of the heavens and the earth and everything that Allāh has created" such as the sun, the moon, the shooting stars, the orbiting planets, the blowing winds, and the surging seas; receiving the knowledge of how things are formed and give birth, one to the other. When their thoughts become immersed in this, the light of gnosis will begin to appear in their heart by way of reflection on the divine actions.

الأصل التاسع المشاهدة وأنواعها وتقاسيمها

اعلم أن من قام بوظيفة تعلم العلم الشرعي فقد كمل فطرته العقلية ومن قام بالعمل بالعلم ظاهرا فقد كمل فطرته الجبلية النفسية ومن قام بحق المراقبة لله عز وجل في قلبه فقد كمل فطرته القلبية ويبقى عليه تكميل فطرته الروحية وذلك فتح يفتحه الله تعالى على عباده المحبين له المشتاقين إليه الطالبين قربه المهتدين بذلك ليلهم ونهارهم كاهتمام الفقيه بالتفقه أو أشد.

فإذا سار العبد في هذه الطريقة المذكورة من تأدية حق المحاسبة والمراقبة ووصل من ظاهره إلى باطنه واستقام الظاهر بالمحاسبة والباطن بالمراقبة وصفا القلب وسكن واطمأن بالتقوى الكاملة والزهد الكامل فهنالك يرجى للعبد أن يتداركه الحق عز وجل بجذبته ويطلع على قلبه نجوم العلم به وأقمار توحيده وشموس معرفته.

ولا ينضبط ما ينادي به الحق عباده وأهل ولايته لكن ترتيب المشاهد على مقتضى الترتيب العلمي ثلاثة أقسام معرفة الله عز وجل في أفعاله ومعرفته في صفاته ومعرفته به عز وجل.

الأول أن يفتح للقلب التفكر في نعم الله عز وجل وآلائه وصنائعه وصنعه وخلقه وأمره فيتفكر ﴿في ملكوت السماوات والأرض وما خلق الله من شيء﴾ من الشمس والقمر والنجوم السائرة والأفلاك الدائرة والرياح الذارية والبحار المتلاطمة ويفتح له علم التكوين والتوليد للأشياء بعضها من بعض فإذا استغرقت فكرته في هذا بدا على سره نور المعرفة بواسطة الفكر في الأفعال

This is called gnosis of Allāh ﷻ by way of divine action which is superior to mere faith in Him. It is something which encounters the heart, which becomes filled with it and impacted by it in a manner which cannot be removed.

The second is gnosis of divine attributes. This too is revealed in the pure heart when pondering over the divine law, reciting divine revelation composed of commands and prohibitions, promises and threats, and various other things. If the heart becomes immersed in that and swallowed up by its meanings, the lofty spectacle (*mashad al-fauqiyyah*) will appear in their heart, leading to their certainty that this revelation descended from Allāh the Most High, above all things, to Allāh's messenger.

This is called the divine spectacle (*mashad al-ilāhiyyah*). The first one is called the spectacle of lordship (*mashad al-rubūbiyyah*). After that it is likely that the spectacle of communion (*mashad al-maʿiyyah*) will be revealed to the heart; "He is with you wherever you are". As a result, they witness the Magnificent Lord's encompassment of His creation with His knowledge, hearing, and sight, and His proximity to them. This is known as the spectacle of communion.

The third is complete and comprehensive gnosis of all the divine names and attributes' meanings and is the spectacle of assembly (*mashad al-jamʿi*) which brings everything together for the servant. The first spectacles were spectacles of the hearts. This is a spectacle for the souls. With it, the spiritual disposition is perfected, the inner-being is ignited with the light of Allāh's ﷻ exclusive love, and is granted annihilation (*al-fanāʾ*), then permanence (*al-baqāʾ*), then intoxication (*al-sakar*), and then sobriety (*al-ṣawḥu*); as Allāh so provides to His servants which is a blessing He gives to whom He so wills.

Whoever tastes this light a swallow or two is yearning for the taste. Whoever tastes it for an hour or two has truly drank. Whoever is overcome by it to the point that Allāh's ﷻ amassed light fills their veins and joints, has been soaked. They may disappear from that which can be sensed around them, this is intoxication.

فيسمى هذا معرفة الله عز وجل بأفعاله وهو فوق الإيمان به هو شيء يباشر القلب فيمتلئ منه ويتأثر به تأثرا لا يمكنه رفعه.

الثاني معرفة الصفات وذلك ينكشف أيضا في صفاء القلب عند تأمل الشريعة والتلاوة للوحي الإلـهي المتضمن للأمر والنهي والوعد والوعيد وغير ذلك فإذا استغرق القلب وغاب في تلك المعاني بدا على القلب مشهد الفوقية فيوقن حينئذ بأن هذا الوحي نزل من عند الله العلي فوق كل شيء على رسول الله ﷺ.

وسمي هذا مشهد الإلـهية. وذلك الأول يسمى مشهد الربوبية. ثم يرجى أن يكشف للقلب مشهد المعية ﴿وهو معكم أين ما كنتم﴾ فيشهد إحاطة الرب العظيم بخلقه بعلمه وسمعه وبصره وقربه منهم وهذا يسمى مشهد المعية.

الثالث المعرفة الكلية الجامعة لجميع معاني الأسماء والصفات وهو مشهد الجمع يجمع للعبد فيه المتفرقات والمشاهد الأول من مشاهد القلوب وهذا هو مشهد الأرواح فتكمل به الفطر الروحية ويلتهب الباطن بأنوار محبة الله عز وجل الخاصة ويرزق فيه الفناء ثم القاء ثم السكر ثم الصحو لمن رزقه الله تعالى ذلك من عباده وهو فضل الله يؤتيه من يشاء.

فمن ذاق من هذا النور ذوقا نفسا أو نفسين فهو الذائق المشتاق ومن دام له ساعة أو ساعتين فهو الشارب حقا ومن توالى عليه الأمر حتى امتلأت منه عروقه ومفاصله من أنوار الله عز وجل المخزونة فذلك هو الري وربما غاب عن المحسوس فذلك هو السكر

They may wander in various states, discharging them in the image of deeds, which is capacitation (*al-tamkīn*) after censure (*al-talwīn*), sobriety after intoxication. In that process there are numerous varieties of states which cannot be sequenced from the beginning to end such as longing (*al-shawq*), love (*al-ḥub*) , and intimacy (*al-uns*), proximity and connection (*al-qurb wa al-ittiṣāl*), absence and presence (*al-ghaybat wa al-ḥuḍūr*), constriction and expansion (*al-qabḍ wa al-basṭ*), and dispersal and assemblage (*al-tafriqat wa al-jamʿu*).

The one who possesses this final spectacle will have all portions of all the states according to their portion of the witnessing. At this point, the servant will become a servant of Allāh ﷻ, taken over by Allāh in the sense that they have completed their journey and their heart has become attached to Allāh ﷻ in a manner that will never break free. That is the true grasp of the most trustworthy handhold with no break in it from Allāh, not Allāh's messenger ﷺ, resulting in the servant, who comprehends, inheriting a portion of the messenger of Allāh's inner-state, just as they have inherited a portion of his outer knowledge. Thus, they have perfected their disposition in every way and become completely radiant and so, "For the like of this let the workers work" and "for this let the competitors compete" which "is the bounty of Allāh which He gives to whom He wills, and Allāh is the possessor of great bounty".

This marks the completion of the principles, totaling nine in number, upon which the entirety of spiritual wayfaring (*sulūk*), from the beginning to the end, rests. Sufyan once said, "Obtainment will be prevented from those who squander the principles". From that, we have understood that safeguarding these principles is a requisite of obtainment.

The only thing remaining are the supplementary devices which complete spiritual wayfaring, serving it like the various conditions and recommendations of prayer. The principles were like the pillars and obligations; the pillars going uncompensated for with prostration. Success lies with Allāh.

وربما تصرف أحيانا في الأحوال فصرفها في صور الأعمال فذلك هو التمكين بعد التلوين والصحو بعد السكر وفي أثناء ذلك أحوال كثيرة تتنوع لا ينضبط ابتداؤها وانتهاؤها من حال الشوق والحب والأنس والقرب والاتصال والغيبة والحضور القبض والبسط والتفرقة والجمع.

فصاحب هذا المشهد الآخر يكون له من كل حال من الأحوال يصيب على قدر نصيبه من الشهود وهنا يصير العبد عبدا لله عز وجل يتولاه الله عز وجل بمعنى أنه انتهى سيره وسلوكه واتصل قلبه بالله عز وجل اتصالا لا انفصام له واتصل ظاهره بالسنة والمتابعة اتصالا لا انفصام له وذلك هو حقيقة التمسك بالعروة الوثقى التي لا انفصام لها من الله ولا من رسول الله ﷺ فيرث العبد الفقيه قسطا من حال رسول الله ﷺ الباطن كما ورث قسطا من علمه الظاهر فتكمل بذلك فطرته بجميع أجزائها ويتنور بجميع أرجائها و﴿لمثل هذا فليعمل العاملون﴾ وعلى ذلك ﴿فليتنافس المتنافسون﴾ وهو ﴿فضل الله يؤتيه من يشاء والله ذو الفضل العظيم﴾.

فقد كمل الأصول وهي تسعة عليها مدار السلوك من البداية إلى النهاية.

قال سفيان إنما حرموا الوصول بتضييع الأصول. ففهمنا من ذلك أن حفظ الأصول موجب للوصول.

وبقي فصل اللواحق به يتم السلوك وهي بمثابة الهيئات والسنن من الصلاة والأصول بمثابة الأركان والواجبات والأركان لا تجبر بالسجود وبالله التوفيق.

Appendix: Supplementary Spiritual Devices

Part One: Safeguarding One's Temperament within the Capacity of the Journey

They should mind their temperament and its condition. It should be between negligence and excessiveness; neither overly satiated nor extremely famished. It should be balanced, between abstemious and indulgent and between detachment and engagement. There are some who, in the capacity of their journey and spiritual wayfaring, deprive themselves with difficult exercises such as starvation and sleeplessness, possibly abandoning the means out of judiciousness, which results in a deviation of temperament, thus severing their journey. The best nutrition for them is a balanced and moderate diet and avoidance of eating things which produce melancholy such as dry bread all of which are harmful to one's temperament and sever the journey and spiritual wayfaring.

Part Two: Avoidance of Accompanying the Young

Whoever is found to be physically attractive, be they young or with sideburns, can enamor the inner-being, suspending and soiling the intent, thus defiling the heart just as the clothing becomes defiled with impurity. Because the human spirit (*nafs*) is inclined to attractive figures, regardless if the servant intends such or not, and can occur without notice especially for bachelors, so staying away from them is even more stressed due to their need for marriage and potential for desire to form in their heart.

To accompany a ravenous beast of prey is better for them than to live with an attractive youth, even if they are righteous; the harm of the righteous upon the ascetic is worse as they share a connection.

The wayfarer (*sālik*) should therefore stay away from them and the places in which they congregate and live as much as possible. If they are tested with teaching or something similiar, they should be extremely careful.

فصل في اللواحق وهي فصول

الفصل الأول حفظ المزاج في جدة السير والسلوك

فيراعي فيه مزاجه وحاله فيكون بين الإفراط والتفريط فلا يشبع الشبع المفرط ولا يجوع الجوع المفرط فيكون وسطا بين التنعم والتقشف والتجرد والتسبب فبعض الناس لجدة سيره وسلوكه يقطع نفسه بالرياضة الشاقة من الجوع والسهر وربما ترك الأسباب بالأصالة فينحرف مزاجه وينقطع سيره وأنفع الأغذية له الدسم المتوسط بين القليل والكثير وليجتنب أكل الأشياء المولدة للسوداء ومن ذلك الخبز اليابس فكل يضر بالمزاج وينقطع به السير والسلوك.

الفصل الثاني مجانبة صحبة الأحداث

ومن له صورة جميلة تميل إليه النفس حدثا كان أن مختطا فإنه يشغف الباطن ويعلق الهم ويلوثه فيتنجس القلب به كما يتنجس الثوب بنجاسة وذلك من حيث لا يشعر العبد فإن النفس ميلا وارتباطا بالصور الجميلة شاء العبد أو أبى خصوصا للعزبان فإن اجتنابهم في حقهم آكد لفاقتهم إلى النكاح وكمون شهوته في القلب.

ولئن يصحب الإنسان سبعا ضاريا خير له من أن يصحب أو يعاشر أمردا جميلا وإن كان صالحا فضرر الصالح على الناسك أشد لأن بينه وبينه نسبة.

فليتباعد السالك عنهم وعن مواطنهم وعن مجاورتهم مهما أمكن فإن ابتلي بتعليم أو غيره فليكن منه على أشد الحذر.

It should be understood that the objective will not be achieved without a pure venue, if they need to purify their venue, they must stay away from possible contamination.

Part Three: Researching the Sunnah of Allāh's Messenger ﷺ

Including his eating, drinking, sleeping, character, fellowship with his wives and companions, remembrances during mishaps, night prayers, tooth stick (*siwāk*), and purification. After this, they should imitate him as much as possible. After a survey of his life and miracles, the evidence of prophethood will settle in their heart and knowledge of the message and its evidence will serve as a stool upon which monotheism is built. With all of this, compliance will be valid which results in the love of Allāh the Most High, as He ﷻ said, "Say, 'If you love Allāh then follow me and Allāh will love you".

If they read the glorious Qur'ān, they should remember the Prophet ﷺ and will thus witness him in the Qur'ān with his companions, and Allāh ﷻ addressing him and thus they will understand Allāh's commands, prohibitions, and intents as previously mentioned in the etiquettes of prayer. God willing, this will open the heart's pores and through them, with the conferment of Allāh, divine light will flow in.

Part Four: Not Missing Night Prayer at the Time of The Lord's *Nuzūl* to the Worldly Heavens

Whoever consistently prays at that time, even if only two units of prayer, which are lengthy and followed by supplications of forgiveness (if they can do more they should), it is likely that they will be answered and flowing radiance will reach the heart, Allāh willing.

وليعلم أن المقصود لا يحصل إلا مع طهارة المحل ومن افتقر إلى تطهير محله وجب عليه التباعد عن مظان التلوث.

الفصل الثالث مطالعة سنن رسول الله ﷺ

في أكله وشربه ونومه وأخلاقه ومعاشرته لأزواجه ولأصحابه وأذكاره عند الحوادث وتهجده وسواكه وطهوره ثم ليتشبه به مهما أمكنه من ذلك بعد المرور على سيرته ومعجزاته وأيامه فبذلك تقوم شواهد نبوته في قلبه ومعرفة الرسالة بشواهدها كرسي ينبني عليه التوحيد وبجميع ذلك يصح الاتباع ويترتب على الاتباع محبة الله تعالى قال عز من قائل ﴿قل إن كنتم تحبون الله فاتبعوني يحببكم الله﴾.

وإذا قرأ القرآن المجيد يستحضر الرسول ﷺ فيشهد في القرآن مع أصحابه ويشهد مخاطبة الله عز وجل له ثم يفهم عن الله أمره ونهيه ومراده كما تقدم في آداب الصلاة فبذلك إن شاء الله تتفتح مسام القلب وتسري بواسطته الأنوار القدسية إلى القلوب بمعونة الله تعالى وتوفيقه.

الفصل الرابع أن لا يفوته ورده عند الثلث الآخر عند نزول الرب عز اسمه إلى سماء الدنيا

فمن واظب على تهجده في ذلك الوقت ولو بركعتين يطيلهما ويدعو ويستغفر عقيبهما فإن أمكنه أكثر من ذلك كان فإنه يرجى النفوذ ووصول أنوار جارية إلى القلوب إن شاء الله تعالى.

The best time to recite is at night because it is "more effective for concurrence [of heart and tongue] and more suitable for words". At night one's attention is composed and their mind is clear and so they are able to recite while remembering the Glorified in those words, listening to Him and understanding.

Missing out on the night and one's regular litany of prayers demonstrates a lack of interest and misfortune. Most of the fortunate have obtained their share from standing at night and so the seeker (*murīd*) should not miss out in that. If the servant is an aspiring jurist, they should reserve the day for studies and the night to turn to Allāh ﷻ.

Friday should also be made exclusively for Allāh. It is a gauge which measures the servant and all they did during the week. If the previous week was pure, the servant was not tarnished by sin, Friday will be a day of light and abundance. If the week was adulterated, Friday will be gloomy, and they will be met with weariness, fatigue, and disinterest.

Part Five: Continuous Need of Allāh ﷻ

Embarking upon His servitude, relying upon him, entrusting Him, and constantly seeking refuge with Him, which should also occur within the human spirit (*nafs*) if possible.

Sahl said, "Refuge will be based on knowledge of the trial's degree".

This is what servitude of The Sustainer (*ʿubūdiyyat al-Qayyūm*) requires; whose grasp contains our hearts and souls, directing them as He wishes as is reported in the hadith, "O Turner of hearts," or, "O Director of hearts, direct my heart to Your obedience," or, "turn my heart to your obedience".

وأولى الأوقات للتلاوة الليل لأنه ﴿أشد وطئا وأقوم قيلا﴾. وفي الليل يجتمع الهم ويصفو الذهن ويمكن التالي أن يستحضر المتكلم سبحانه في الكلام ثم يسمع منه ويفهم عنه.

ومن فاته الليل وأوراده دل ذلك على برود همته وقلة نصيبه ويقال إن أكثر أهل النصيب إنما حصل لهم النصيب في قيام الليل فينبغي أن لا يفوت المريد ذلك وإن كان العبد متفقها فليجعل نهاره للعلم وليله للتوجه إلى الله عز وجل.

وكذلك يجعل يوم الجمعة لله خالصا فإنه محك يحك العبد به ما مضى من الأسبوع فإذا كان الأسبوع الماضي صافيا لم يدنسه العبد بشيء من المعاصي كان يوم الجمعة يوم الأنوار والمزيد وإن كان قد خلط في الأسبوع كان يوم الجمعة مظلما يجد فيه السآمة والملالة والفتور.

الفصل الخامس دوام الافتقار إلى الله عز وجل

واستعمال العبودية له والتوكل عليه والتفويض إليه ودوام اللجأ إليه وليكن ذلك في الأنفاس إن أمكن.

قال سهل على قدر معرفة الابتلاء يكون الالتجاء.

وهذا هو الذي تقتضيه عبودية القيوم الذي أوراحنا بيده وقلوبنا فهو يصرفها كيف شاء وفي الحديث يا مقلب القلوب أو يا مصرف القلوب صرف قلبي على طاعتك أو قلب قلبي على طاعتك.

Whoever witnesses the subsistence (*al-qayyūmiyyah*) will become attached to Allāh ﷻ in all remaining states for all events, be they good or evil, as the result of His grace or decree. It is therefore a must that we constantly need Allāh the Most High to preserve us in His obedience and protect us from His disobedience. This is a major principle that many are inconsistent with and therefore miss out on much grace.

Some of the shaykhs have said, "Whoever is constantly seeking refuge with Allāh in eating, drinking, coming and going, and in all of their endeavors, Allāh ﷻ will open the door of the spectacles for them, i.e. enlightenment of the inner-being with the radiance of the Magnificent and Sublime".

This is the path to Allāh ﷻ which will connect the servant to Him so long as they are consistent in it. It has been reported in a ḥadīth that the Prophet ﷺ would say, "O Ever-Living, O Sustainer, I call upon you. Do not place me in charge of my soul even for the blinking of an eye. Rectify all of my affairs. There is no deity worthy of worship except you".

This is the last of what is feasible and so all praise belongs to Allāh and may His abundant peace and prayers be upon our master Muḥammad, his family, and companions.

ومن شهد القيومية تعلق بالله عز وجل في سائر الأحوال فإن الحوادث كلها من خير وشر هي من نتائج فضله أو أقضيته فيجب علينا دوام الافتقار إلى الله تعالى ليحفظنا في طاعته ويحرسنا عن معصيته وهذا أصل كبير تخلف عنه قوم ففاتهم به فضل كثير.

قال بعض المشائخ من أدام الالتجاء إلى الله تعالى في أكله وشربه وتقلباته وحركاته فتح الله عز وجل عليه باب المشاهد وهو تنوير الناطن بأنوار العظمة والجلال.

فهذا طريق موصل إلى الله عز وجل بنفسه إذا واظب العبد عليه وفي الحديث كان رسول الله ﷺ يقول يا حي يا قيوم برحمتك أستغيث لا تكلني إلى نفسي طرفة عين وأصلح لي شأني كله لا إله إلا أنت.

وهذا آخر ما تيسر والحمد لله وحده وصلى الله على سيدنا محمد وآله وصحبه وسلم تسليما كثيرا.

About the Translator

John Starling is an alumnus of NCSU's Poole College of Management and the Islamic University of Madinah's College of Islamic Doctrine and Mission. He holds a Master's Degree in Islamic Studies from the Islamic University of Minnesota, has been granted a general/comprehensive ijāzah by Shaykh Dr. Muṭlaq al-Jāsir with permission to award ijāzahs and chains of narration, and is currently pursuing a Master's Degree in Nonprofit Management and Philanthropy.

About the Translation

The translation of this text is based on the first edition print published by Dār al-Bashā'ir al-Islāmi in 2002 which was supported by the verification and commentary of Shaykh Walīd b. Muḥammad b. ʿAbdullah al-ʿAlawi. This was the only edition readily available.

The arduous task of retyping the Arabic text was undertaken to benefit the Arabic student and translation enthusiast.

Translating this work and other works of the Ḥanbali School is an honor of a lifetime. For that, all praise and thanks belong to Allāh the Mighty and Sublime.

To best represent the works of this tradition, suggestions and corrections are welcome and greatly appreciated.

To find other book titles, courses, how-to guides, and a growing repository of questions and answers according to the school, visit hanbalidisciples.com.

Made in the USA
Middletown, DE
15 November 2020

24142926R00050